1

FROM THE LEAST TO THE GREATEST

DR. PHILLIP M. JACKSON

TABLE OF CONTENTS

ACKNOWLEDGEMENTS

To my Lord and Savior Jesus Christ, thank you for dying for my sins and saving my soul. Many thanks to my committee for all of your support and encouragement: Dr. Connie S. Peterson, my Chairperson and Advisor; Dr. Williams C. Morris, Founder and Chancellor and Dr. Peter Harvey, Instructor. I appreciate the learning opportunity provided by my committee.

To my son Corey Maurice Jackson and my caring, loving, and supportive wife Ledia S. Jackson whom I love, appreciate, and adore. You are consistently there for me through the thick and thin and I love you more and more each day.

I cannot forget to thank Minister Rickey L. Curry for encouraging me to go back to school; it has been a blessing. I am forever grateful to be blessed with a loving and caring family, thank you for your support. And, finally, to my daughters in Christ, Sister Laketha Wilson and Sister Candice Johnson who thought it not robbery to work around my busy schedule and help me complete

this project. My heartfelt thanks to all.

DEDICATION:

In the 50 years that God has allowed to me to be on this Earth, I have accomplished a lot. I have been in places where I am convinced was only due to the favor that God has bestowed upon my life. Not only have I been in some remarkable places, but there have been remarkable people that have dealt a hand in me becoming the man of God I am today.

I would first like to give honor and thanks to God, the very reason I am here. I don't care about the wealth that I may accumulate or the fame my name may bring; I will always remain a poor man in need of God. He is my everything, the source of my strength. It is because of Him that I live and breathe. Even as I write this, I am having a David moment. If I had ten thousand tongues, I still could not thank Him enough.

To my wonderful mother, Vallie Lee Lock, I am grateful for all that you have done for me, not only when I was growing up, but now. Sometimes I have hurt secretly, and you have felt my pain and have moved like only a mother would. And for that I am eternally thankful. To the late Robert Edward Jackson, my father, who taught me the importance of being a "real" father. The lesson you taught me on giving is one that I will operate in until I reach glory. To my grandparents, uncles, aunts, sisters, and brother, I sincerely say, "Thank you".

To my father-in-law the late District Evangelist Willie Daniels, not only were you my father-in-law, but my spiritual father as well. Sometimes I wish you could see a glimpse of all that your baby girl and I have accomplished, not so much in the natural but in the spiritual realm. And please know that your legacy shall live on. Holiness is still right, and holy I shall live until we meet again. Church Mother Queen Esther Daniels, my mother- in-law, a powerful, powerful woman of God. I can hear you singing your song in my head, "The older I get, the sweeter I want to be". I thank God for you all so much, for the teaching, the guidance, the laying on hands, and also trusting me with your daughter – she has been a blessing unto me.

The Saints of Empowering Tabernacle House of Prayer Outreach Ministry Apostolic Faith, I thank every one of you all. Thank you for your faithfulness, thank you for your patience. Trust me when I tell you all, pay day is coming after a while.

Last but certainly not least, my wonderful wife, Church Mother Ledia S. Jackson. Honey, I believe we are the dynamic duo. I thank you for being my helpmeet. Thank you for encouraging me when tough times came. Thank you for staying in tune with God and obeying His voice when He spoke. A lot of the moves that you made helped to bless our home, and I thank you so much for that. You make the scriptures in Proverb 31 come to life, because you are that virtuous woman. We are in this for the long haul – Love you to life!!!

I could not conclude this dedication without mentioning my son, the late Corey Maurice Jackson. Son, life has not been the same since you have been gone, but I still glorify God. Sometimes me and your mom sit around and talk for hours about how things would have been if you were still here. We talk about the grandchildren we would have had running around the house. It is no secret son, we miss you! We thank God for strength because that's how we are able to continue on. We will forever keep your memory alive! Love you, Corey!

~ In Loving Memory of Corey Maurice Jackson ~

INTRODUCTION: FROM THE LEAST TO THE GREATEST:

When someone often speaks of the word "greatest" it is always compared to natural accomplishments that are accompanied by materialist items such as cars, expensive homes, and lavish living. My hope is to display what it really means to be viewed as "greatest" and that tangible items gives the proper definition of this word absolutely no value.

When examining the life of many leaders in the Bible, it is greatly illuminated what it takes to wear a title of that caliber. Let's take the Apostle Paul for example, when Paul operated under the name of Saul he killed many people who served God. But one day, Paul's time as being a servant to sin expired and God called his name. The Bible lets us know that as Saul was traveling to Damascus a bright light surrounded him coming from Heaven. The Lord spoke directly to Saul – Acts 9:4 "… Saul, Saul, why persecutes thou me"? From that day forward, life for Saul, whose name was later changed to Paul, was never the same. He became a fearless man of

God. Paul was considered as one that was born out of due season, but out of the twenty-seven books in the New Testament, Paul attributed to thirteen of them. To some, reading Paul's resume and learning all the harm he had done to God's people redemption would seem impossible. That is why we glorify God for grace and mercy because those factors see beyond the filth and zooms in on the gold.

I, like Paul, did deplorable things as I dipped and dodged the calling that God had upon my life. As God began to do a transformation in my life, many could not see the good, for focusing on my past. But I am so glad that God does not look at what we come from, He looks at where He can take us. Through this book, I plan to use the lives of influential Biblical figures who were viewed as being the least, but God elevated to the greatest. I will also use various parts of my life as an illustration of how tough things can get in our way on this journey, but how it' imperative that we continue to strive faithfully in God, holding fast to one of my favorite sayings, "Pay Day is

Coming After While".

CHAPTER 1

THE LIFE OF JOSEPH

How many of life's lessons have you had to learn 'the hard way'? I've certainly learned a few that way myself. They make for great testimonies–if you can survive them. I've discovered, that there's a better way. God's Word is full of good and bad experiences of men and women of old, placed there as examples for you and me. I decided a long time ago that a study of those examples is a much better and a lot less painful way to learn. Through the study of their lives, I have gained the wisdom and understanding to make decisions that have allowed me to avoid many of the hard knocks that come through trial and error. 1 Corinthians 10:11 says, "Now all these things happened unto them for ensamples (examples): and they are written for our admonition, upon whom the ends of the world are come". One of my favorite studies in the Bible is the life of Joseph. Joseph was a man who possessed godly character and integrity.

His life's story is one that I consider to be of the least to

the greatest.

Joseph was the eleventh son of Jacob, and his story can be found in Genesis 37:50. It all began with a dream at the age of seventeen.....Joseph knew the dreams he was having were from the Lord, and that they revealed God's purpose and plan for his life Genesis 37:6-7 and 9 says, And he said unto them, Hear, I pray you, this dream which I have dreamed: For, behold, we were binding sheaves in the field, and, lo, my sheaf arose, and also stood upright; and, behold, your sheaves stood round about, and made obeisance to my sheaf. And he dreamed yet another dream, and told it his brethren, and said, Behold, I have dreamed a dream more; and, behold, the sun and the moon and the eleven stars made obeisance to me. Joseph believed what the Lord had spoken to him, and immediately announced it to his family: God told me that all of you will bow down to me someday! Some people believe that Joseph made a fatal mistake when he shared his vision. But I believe that he was so excited about hearing from God that he just had to tell it. However, this bold announcement only served to draw his father's rebuke and feed his brothers' growing hatred (www.gotquestions.org).

Joseph had heard from God. He now had a

purpose and vision for his life, even if it wasn't received

by others. We were all created for a divine purpose as

well. God may not speak to you in a dream, but if you will

14

become determined to know His plan for your life, He will reveal it to you. The Bible makes it very clear in Ephesians 5:17 where it says," Wherefore be ye not unwise, but understanding what the will of the Lord is".

Not only will the pursuit of your vision bring fulfillment, but it will also keep you on track. Joseph's vision kept him on track during very difficult times of his life and when faced with great temptation.

> The beginning of a dream often generates more enthusiasm than wisdom. We say things we shouldn't say and do things we shouldn't do. Like Joseph, we sometimes do not start off well. But, unlike Joseph, too often we give up on our dreams in the early stages when they are most fragile. Joseph encourages us to recapture the dream we abandoned and once again claim it as our own. The Bible says that when Joseph told his family about his dream, his father responded, "What is this dream that you have dreamed? Shall your mother and I and your brothers indeed come to bow down to the earth before you?" (Genesis 37:10) Clearly, Joseph wasn't going to get the support from anyone in his family. It is very difficult to retain your dream when your family wants you to release it. But when your dream comes from God, the dream holds you when you feel unable to hold it. Just because things don't go as planned, that's no reason to give up (Maxwell: 29-30).

Your purpose – God-given dream-will inspire you, motivate you, and help restrain your flesh in the absence of any evidence that it's coming to pass. Don't be surprised if some of your most forceful opposition comes from those closest to you. It did for Joseph. Joseph knew what God had spoken and declared about him was true no matter what the circumstances indicated. Genesis 39:2 defies the logic of Joseph's circumstances. It says, "And the Lord was with Joseph, and he was a prosperous man; and he was in the house of his master the Egyptian". God's Word clearly states that Joseph was a prosperous man. This was at a time in his life when he was serving as a slave. His brothers had sold him into slavery and told his father that he was dead. No longer the wealthy, well-dressed, favorite son, Joseph found himself in a foreign land, stripped of everything. His rich Egyptian master stood beside him with all of the extravagance that came with abundant wealth, but the Bible forever records Joseph as being the truly prosperous one.

God views prosperity much differently than we do. Material things are not indicative of prosperity. True prosperity is knowing that God is with you and keeping His vision alive in your heart. True prosperity is not having a lot of money, but it is God's favor, anointing, and power at work in your life to obtain it. Deuteronomy 8:18 says, "Thou shalt remember the Lord thy God: for it is He that giveth thee power to get wealth that He may establish His covenant". Joseph believed he was prosperous because he knew prosperity came from God, not man. He had something on the inside that was not affected by his circumstances, and it enabled Joseph to operate in faith. Instead of grumbling and complaining, Joseph served others and ministered wholeheartedly to their needs. As he diligently labored, God blessed the work of his hands. If Joseph could do it, so can you and I. We have the same power dwelling on the inside of us that raised Jesus from the dead. Begin to see yourself as God sees you, a prosperous person, regardless of your physical circumstances. Recognize and acknowledge the fact that God is with you, that you are anointed and highly favored. Serve others with all your heart as unto the Lord. Eliminate murmuring and complaining, and replace them with praise and thanksgiving, knowing that God will complete what He has begun in your life.

Joseph maintained his integrity, recognizing the favor and presence of God in his life. Joseph lived a God-dependent life, and he lived it in the midst of great adversity. He knew his future rested in the hands of the Lord. Psalm 75:6-7 says, "For promotion cometh neither from the east, nor from the west, nor from the south. But God is the judge: he putteth down one, and setteth up another". Joseph's stint in Potiphar's employ gave him a wide range of fiduciary responsibilities. At first, Joseph was just a mere servant in his master's house. But when Potiphar recognized Joseph's general competence, he promoted him to be his personal steward and "put him in charge of all that he had" (Genesis: 39:4). After a time, Potiphar's wife took a sexual interest in Joseph (Genesis: 39:7). Joseph's refusal of the wife's advances was articulate and reasonable. He reminded her of the broad trust that Potiphar had placed in him and described the relationship she sought was wicked and sinful against God (Genesis: 39:9). He was sensitive to both the social and theological dimensions. Furthermore, he offered his verbal resistance repeatedly, and he even avoided being in her presence. When physically assaulted, Joseph made the choice to flee half-naked rather than to submit to sin. The sexual harassment by Potiphar's wife took place in a power relationship that disadvantaged Joseph. "Although she believed that she had a right to use Joseph in this way, her words and contact were clearly unwelcoming to him" (www.gotquestions.org). Joseph's work required him to be at home where she was, yet he could not call the matter to Potiphar's attention without interfering in their marital relationship. Even after his escape and arrest on false charges, Joseph seems to have had no legal recourse.

The facets of Joseph's episode touch closely on the issues of sexual harassment in the workplace today. People have different standards of what counts for inappropriate speech and physical contact, but the whims of those in power are what often count in practice.

Workers are often expected to report incidences of potential harassment to their superiors, but often are reluctant to do so because they know the risk of obscurity and retaliation. To compound this, even when harassment can be documented, workers may suffer for having come forward. Joseph's godliness did not rescue him from false accusation and imprisonment. If we find ourselves in a parallel situation, our godliness is no guarantee that we will escape unscathed. But Joseph did leave an instructive testimony to Potiphar's wife and possibly others in the household. Knowing that we belong to the Lord and that He defends the weak will certainly help us to face difficult situations without giving up.

Joseph's life was about to take another turn. His dependence on God would open a door that would literally change history and become an even greater display of his character. As his story continues, Joseph now finds himself in prison. The chief butler and the chief baker of the king of Egypt offended their king who then had them thrown in prison with Joseph. There, they both had a dream but no one to interpret them (Genesis 40:1-

7). Joseph demonstrated his trust and dependence in the Lord by stating, "Do not interpretations belong to God? Tell me them, I pray you" (Genesis 40:8).The Lord gave Joseph the interpretation, and both came to pass. The butler kept his job, and the baker lost his head. In spite of the miracle of these interpretations, the butler said nothing of Joseph for two years. Most people would have given up, but not Joseph; he knew God's plan would be fulfilled.

Then the Pharaoh himself had a dream that all the magicians of Egypt could not interpret. God was about to take Joseph from rags to riches in one inspired moment. When the king learned of Joseph's ability to interpret dreams, he sent for him and asked if he could interpret his dreams. Joseph was ready. He confidently answered in Genesis 41:16 saying, "It is not in me: God shall give Pharaoh an answer of peace". Joseph, by the Spirit, interpreted the king's dream. Equally as important, the king realized the Spirit of God was in Joseph. His response is recorded in Gen. 41:39-40, which says, "And Pharaoh said unto Joseph, Forasmuch as God hath shewed thee all this, there is none so discreet and wise as thou art: Thou shalt be over my house, and according unto thy word shall all my people be ruled: only in the throne will I be greater than thou". Promotion had truly come from God. Immediately, Joseph found himself promoted to a position of power, second only to Pharaoh. It's important to understand that Joseph had either been serving as a slave or was imprisoned for seventeen years after the time that his purpose was revealed and before it was fulfilled. It's so tempting to become weary or impatient and abandon the vision for an easier way. But don't do it, and you'll reap. Galatians 6:9 says, "And let us not be weary in well doing: for in due season we shall reap, if we faint not". If you continue to read in Genesis, you will find that Joseph remained dependent on God, and he never lost his way in the midst of such power and wealth. He kept his God-given vision alive, served others wholeheartedly, and remained totally dependent on God. Why? Because he had a vision that had not yet been fulfilled. God was going to use this slave to save his family and a nation.

It was nine years from the time Joseph was placed in power before his brothers came to Egypt seeking help. Think of the options that were available to Joseph. If he wanted revenge, he could have taken it. He could have acted in pride and demanded an audience with his father and brothers, humiliating them and forcing them to bow before him. But Joseph did nothing; he refused to act in the flesh and remained dependent on God. How many of us would have exercised that kind of restraint? Not many. Through Joseph's example, I've recognized the importance of seeking God even more when things are going well. Prosperity and success will test your character infinitely more than hardship! When you're in trouble and your back is against the wall, you know you need help. But did you know that success has corrupted more individuals than hardship ever has? It's prosperity that often causes people to lose sight of their God-given vision or to attempt to bring it to pass through their own natural ability. "Even with extreme wealth and power at his disposal, Joseph waited on the Lord and watched in faith as He brought the dream to fulfillment" (www.gotquestions.org). And when Joseph came home, they (his brethren) brought him the present which was in their hand into the house, and bowed themselves to him to the earth (Genesis 43:26).

The story of Joseph is powerful – full of wisdom and truth. I believe every Christian needs to study his story again and again. His story is a realistic recognition that standing up to sexual harassment may have devastating consequences. Yet, it is also a story of hope that by God's grace, good may eventually prevail in the situation. Joseph also provides a model for us, that even when we are falsely accused and wrongly treated, we must carry on with the work God has given us, allowing God to make it right in the end.

In a town by the name of Jennings, Florida, many people already speculate that much can't come from here (sounds familiar). They believe you have to move hundreds of miles away just to become successful. Once success comes, many forget where they even came from. Well, my story is quite different. I can remember always being exposed to church. From me trying to sing in the church choir, (but being kicked out because of my behavior) to listening to my mom playing a variety of gospel music around the house. Even as a young child, I would grab a book, preach out of that book to my sisters, then close the book and pass around a plate to collect the offering. Many didn't understand the calling that God had over my life, and to be quite honest, I didn't either.

I can recall being a senior in high school, and not to boast or brag, but I was one of the best football players in this area. I had so many offers to attend schools both near and far. I was a small man in stature, but I could easily bench press 450 pounds. Sounds crazy I know, but I was a beast. Then all of a sudden, the call that God had on my life became so real. I, the jock of Hamilton County, the one that was a beast on the field, the one that possessed leadership skills like no one else, overdosed on horse tranquilizer. Scholarships began to get taken away; people began to formulate all types of predictions about my life and football, as I knew it, was over. While many were wondering, "What is PJ going to do now?" I was making a vow to God. I told God that if he could just simply save my life, that I would serve Him with everything that was within me. I learned something very important about making a vow, even when we forget about the words that our mouths have uttered in shear desperation, God never forgets. And in my case, God never forgot.

Now I didn't go from recovery (from that horrible accident) to the church. I'd be lying if I said that I did. I was carrying pistols, snorting cocaine and could have had any woman that I wanted. Sometimes, I would be so high that all I could do was come home and lay across my mother's bed telling her just how high I was and begging her to cook me something to eat, because one time I almost burned the house down. I also had a very quick temper. I didn't mess with people, but if they messed with me, I would seriously try to hurt them, and that's no lie. So, people looking at my actions were saying that I wouldn't live to be twenty-five. They adamantly proclaimed that I was one of the worst children in our family. Honestly, people had counted me out, but I am so thankful that God saw otherwise.

I became involved with a young lady that came out of the "sanctified church" (as people would call them). Her father was a pastor, and her mother was the church mother. Above all of that, she was a clean and pure young lady. Sometimes, I would go look in the window of their church and watch those people dance and shout and cry. To me, back then, that was kind of funny. But she would come to the house, and my mother would let her come in the back room (and that was something that my mother was usually against). She would comb my hair, pick out something for me to wear, then she would take me church. She wasn't looking at who I was or the things that I did, but her mother taught her that if she wanted me as a husband then she needed to keep me in church. As a result of us getting involved with one another, she blessed me with a handsome son, Corey Maurice Jackson. Even in the midst of all of that, God was still pulling me in. Approximately a year after Corey was born, Mrs. Ledia Daniels Jackson and I got married. I turned my life over to the Lord, and that's when I really began to live life. Life was not in the weed that I was smoking, or the cocaine that I was snorting, or even in the pistols that I was carrying, but life was in my humbly submitting to the will of God. I would love to say once the conversion took place that my life became so easy, but it didn't. I became a faithful member of St. Paul House of Prayer; whatever my father-in- law (my Pastor) needed me to do, I did it. The same zeal I had in the world; God transformed it in me for His use. Before I knew it, I was operating as an Elder in the church. Then when my father-in-law passed away, I became the Assistant Pastor of St. Paul House of Prayer with Pastor Kenneth S. Daniels being my Pastor. My wife, our son, and I were living the life. Corey had grown up to be a handsome, respectful, and outstanding athlete. I was so proud to be his father. I couldn't go to many of his games because of my duties with the ministry, but I was still one of his biggest fans. Then one night, April 4th, 2006 to be exact, our lives changed forever. We received a call saying that our Corey, 20 years old, had been killed in a car accident, and someone had to come and identify his body. I knew that day that if my wife and I didn't have a relationship with God, we would have lost our mind. Our only child gone, no more watching him come in the house and fix a big bowl of cereal and just talking to me and his mom. Those days would be no more. I can honestly say, that was the most hurting experience that I ever encountered. But God. After we buried our son, we put up tents and held tent revivals. I began to move for God like never before, because I knew that if I let an ounce of depression set in, the enemy was waiting to have his way in my life. I began to church like a wild man. And in 2007, the Lord called me to establish a church of my very own and to name it: Empowering Tabernacle House of Prayer Outreach Ministry Apostolic Faith. I began to watch God take me from least in the kingdom to the greatest!

CHAPTER 2

THE TRANSITION: GREATNESS IN TRAINING

We can learn a lot from the life of David. Scripture says, "He was a man after God's own heart" (1 Samuel 13:13-14; Acts 13:22)! We are first introduced to David, after Saul was made king at the insistence of the people (1 Samuel 8:5, 10:1). This choice of king, or even having an earthly king at all, was against the will of God, and although Saul was anointed by God through Samuel, he did not measure up as God's king. While King Saul was making one mistake on top of another, God sent Samuel to find His chosen shepherd, David, the son of Jesse (1 Samuel 16:10, 13). David was believed to be 12-16 years of age when he was called in from tending his father's sheep to be anointed as the true king of Israel. As soon as the anointing oil flowed down David's head, the Spirit of the Lord departed from King Saul (1 Samuel 16:14). The fact that evil spirits were tormenting Saul brought David into the king's service (1 Samuel 16:21). Saul was pleased with young David, but this feeling vanished quickly as David rose in strength to slay the Philistine giant, Goliath, and win the overwhelming favor of the people (1 Samuel 17:45-51). The chant in the camp of Saul was taunting as the people sang out the praises of David and demeaned their king, causing a raging jealousy in Saul that never subsided (1 Samuel 18:7-8).

"If you or someone you know has eked his way through life amid strife, conflict and continuous battles, then you might understand how David lived and felt throughout his lifetime" (www.gotquestions.org). Although Saul never stopped pursuing him with the intent to kill him, David never raised a hand against his king and God's anointed (1 Samuel 19:1-2, 24:5-7). He did, however, raise up a mighty army and with power from God defeated everyone in his path, always asking God first for permission and instructions before going into battle (2 Samuel 5:22-23, 23:8-17). Throughout the life of David, God honored and rewarded this unconditional obedience of His servant and gave him success in everything he did (2 Samuel 8:6). David mourned King Saul's death and put to death the one claiming responsibility for it (2 Samuel 1:12-16). Only after Saul's death was David anointed king over the house of Judah

(2 Samuel 2:4), and even then, he had to fight against

the house of Saul before being anointed king over Israel

at the age of thirty (2 Samuel 5:3-4). Now king, David

conquered Jerusalem and became more and more

powerful because the Lord Almighty was with him (2

Samuel 5:7). David was so enthralled with bringing the

Ark of the Covenant to Jerusalem that he omitted some

of God's instructions on how to transport the Ark and who

was to carry it. This resulted in the death of Uzzah who,

amid all the celebrations, reached out to steady the Ark,

when God struck him down, and he died there beside it

(2 Samuel 6:1-7). In fear of the Lord, David abandoned

the moving of the Ark for three months and let it rest in

the house of Obed-Edom (2 Samuel 6:11). After the Ark

was in its rightful place, David decided to build a temple

of the Lord around it (2 Samuel 6:17). Because of David's

bloody, battle-scarred record as well as his adulterous

relationship with Bathsheba and the slaying of her

husband, God denied his otherwise faithful servant the

honor of building the temple, the house of the Lord (2

Samuel 6:5-14). This was surely a blow to David, but God assured him He would continue to make his name the greatest on the earth and forever establish the throne of David through David's son, Solomon. Instead of being angry with God and having a pity party, David sat before the Lord, praising Him and thanking Him for all the many blessings he had received in his life (2 Samuel 7:18-29). David's battles did not end with his kingship but continued with the surrounding nations and within his own household. Throughout the life of David, His sons connived and conspired to take control of the kingdom and they, as did Saul, threatened their own father's life. As with the death of Saul, David mourned the death of his beloved son Absalom, showing a passionate and forgiving heart (2 Samuel chapters 15-18). David's broken heart and contrite spirit are what brought him the forgiveness of God and are what will bring him back to be the prince of Christ during Christ's millennial reign.

Below are 5 Lessons we can learn from the Life of David:

Number 1: A Heart for God Prepares Us to Be Used by God:

David is chosen to be king because he has what Saul does not: a heart for God. 1 Samuel 13:14 says the Lord "sought out a man after his own heart" to be king, and Saul simply was not this man. When Samuel goes to anoint the new king of Israel, he assumes David's strong and noble oldest brother must be the chosen one. However, God tells Samuel not to focus on physical prowess: "Do not look on his appearance or on the height of his stature, because I have I rejected him. For the LORD sees not as man sees: man looks on the outward appearance, but the LORD looks on the heart" (1 Samuel 16:7). David's heart for God prepares him to be used by God. Our impressive resumes aren't what make us useful in God's kingdom. The first lesson we learn from David's life is the importance of cultivating a heart for God above all else.

Number 2: The Spirit of God Equips Us to Do the Will of God:

The lives of David and Saul make it crystal clear that if we want to do God's will, we must be filled with the Spirit. Although Saul is filled with the Spirit and actually prophesies early in his public life, his disobedience causes the Spirit to depart from him and instead "rush upon David" (1 Samuel 16:13-14). Without the Spirit, we are powerless to fulfill the role to which God has called us as Christians. The Spirit enables us to obey God. The Bible assures us that if we "walk by the Spirit", we won't "gratify the desires of the flesh" (Galatians 5:16). And the Spirit's presence in us results in fruit which makes us effective in ministry: "love, joy, peace, peace, patience, kindness, goodness, faithfulness, gentleness, self-control" (Galatians 5:22-23). That is why we must pray to be filled with the Spirit (Ephesians 5:18).

Number 3: It's Better to Fear God than to Be Nine Feet Tall:

David's defeat of Goliath is one of the most vivid examples of what fear of God can accomplish. David feared God more than he feared Goliath, so he was not intimidated by this nine-foot giant before him. David believed the promises of God more than he feared Goliath. The Lord had promised the Israelites that they would conquer the Philistines, and David trusted him. God wants this same kind of fear to be a part of our lives. If we fear God more than anyone or anything else, we will be able to obey and please him in powerful ways. Of course, David is really a picture of the Greater Champion Jesus Christ. David defeated the enemy and delivered a nation—in one battle for a short time. Jesus Christ defeated the enemy—the devil, sin, and death—and delivered his people for all time. That leads us to the next lesson we learn from David.

Number 4: The Glory of David is not about David - It's about Jesus:

David's life is one example of the many pointers and prophecies that speak of Jesus Christ throughout the Old Testament. In David's "last words" in 2 Samuel 23:1-7, he alludes to Jesus several times. He first calls himself "the anointed of the God of Jacob" (2 Samuel 23:1). David was the "anointed" because Samuel anointed him with oil and because God anointed him with the Holy Spirit (1 Samuel 16:13). But "anointed" in Hebrew is Messiah, and in

Greek it is Christ. *David is pointing to the Greater Christ. This is the significance of Peter's answer to Jesus in Matthew 16:15-16: "He said to them, 'But who do you say that I am?' Simon Peter replied, 'You are the Christ, the Son of the living God." Jesus is also the fulfillment of what David calls "the everlasting covenant" (2 Samuel 23:5): When your days are fulfilled and you lie down with your fathers, I will raise up your offspring after you, who shall come from your body, and I will establish his kingdom. 13 He shall build a house for my name, and I will establish the throne of his kingdom forever 2 Samuel 7:12-13. This is no human figure. Solomon, Hezekiah, Josiah - the greatest kings of Israel lived at best 70 or 80 years. None of them had an eternal kingdom. This is Jesus Christ, the Son of David, who is the King above all kings who will live and reign forever.*

Number 5: Sin Can Bring Horrible Consequences, but Sin Can Be Forgiven:

1-2 Samuel show that sin can result in horrible consequences: Eli the priest fails to fear God and his two sons are killed because of it. Saul fails to obey and honor God, and the kingdom is given to another man. But David's sin against Bathsheba shows this most vividly of all. When David takes Bathsheba and kills her husband Uriah, he sins in so many ways, and the Lord is not silent or indifferent to them. In fact, he promises to bring "the sword" upon David's house, and that sword takes four of his sons. Such sobering consequences for sin are meant to cause us to fear falling into sin. But there is forgiveness in the life of

David as well. After Nathan the prophet confronts David for his sin, David confesses. Nathan then speaks the forgiveness of God: "The LORD has put away your sin; you shall not die" (2 Samuel 12:13). David's true repentance is matched by the Lord's forgiveness. And in the end, God's forgiveness far surpasses any consequences we might experience. Consequences can only last for a lifetime, but forgiveness lasts forever. When we stand before God in the new heavens and new earth, our sins and their aftermath will be behind us and only life and joy in the presence of a merciful savior will be ahead. Such forgiveness is ours when we believe in Jesus Christ, the one who forever and completely takes our sins away (Hebrews 10:1-18). David's life teaches us not to take the glorious reality of God's mercy for granted (www.gotquestions.org).

When a lot of people think about training, it seems to leave a bad taste in their mouth, especially when the training exceeds a day or two. They began to raise the question(s), "Is all of the training really necessary? Does it really take all of this?" And if they are not careful, they will quit before their training session is finished. The price tag for the priesthood of Believers is a trained church body. I am not talking about college degrees or scholarly accreditation. I am talking about spiritual training. The

New Testament qualifications for ministry (see Acts 6:3 and 1Timothy 3:1-13) focus on spiritual maturity, not on intellect or academic accomplishments. What is involved in spiritual training, spiritual maturity, and spiritual formation? A large portion of it is the basics of prayer and Bible study. We must remain in constant communication with our Lord. This takes time, self-discipline, patience and intentional planning. We often admire the great works of faith done by Jesus. We are awed by the decisions He made to serve others; most notably His willingness to sacrifice Himself to ransom all humanity. And we want to be like Jesus. It has even become popular in some circles to ask, What would Jesus do?

All this is good. "But, as Dallas Willard points out in his book *The Spirit of the Disciplines,* it is a mistake to try to imitate the heroic moments of Jesus without also trying to imitate the lifestyle that laid the foundations for those heroic moments — specifically a lifestyle that included much prayer, a willingness to be alone with God" (www.gotquestions.org).

One strategy of Satan is to keep us so busy with activity that we don't have time to listen to God.

Sometimes we are so busy doing stuff, some of it supposedly for God that we cut ourselves off from God. We are like Martha when we should be like Mary, listening to Jesus. "Jesus trained His disciples not so much through formal activities, but more by osmosis" (MacArthur: 75). They were with Him as He ministered, and they saw not just what He did, but also the flavor in which He did it — the flavor of compassion, not compulsion. We also need to be trained through spending time with the Lord, in prayer and study. That will lead us to activity, to be sure, but on God's timetable and not based on our impatient desire to 'do something'. If our works, or lack of them, is taking us away from God, we need to realize that we are not working for God, and we need to change our ways. His purpose is to draw us closer to Himself, to fulfill the real goal of conforming us to the image of Christ. Patience is a fruit of the Holy Spirit, often lacking in human nature. We are reluctant to wait upon the Lord. We are frustrated when things don't move as fast as we want them to. We are racing from here to there in a great frenzy, thinking that speed or busyness is a measure of success, but we are not getting anywhere in particular.

As the saying goes, if we do not know where we are going, we might end up someplace else. Sometimes we need to stop racing around and spend some time getting our bearings. Others have made no motions in any direction. This is true spiritually, as well as physically. Every day, we need to spend time with the Lord, and his instruction book, to get our bearings. This takes discipline, patience, and time for osmosis to do its work. We need to let it soak into our lives and habits. There are no short-cuts available. "Indeed, it is God who must be our vision, our all in all, the treasure that we seek. He is the goal, not some project or activity" (www.gotquestions.org). No matter how good the activity may be, we must ensure that we don't become so preoccupied with it that we have less and less time for God Himself. So I want to emphasize again our need for daily prayer and study. Let us drink deeply of the water of life, Jesus Christ. Let His thoughts fill our thoughts. Let us fellowship with Him in prayer and study, not with a focus on what we want, but with a willingness to learn what He wants for us.

If we accept Jesus as Lord, we let Him be the Lord of our lives. We let Him be the Master of our behavior, the Master of our feelings, the Master of our mind. When we accept Him as Lord, we commit ourselves to His purpose, His way of life, and His teachings. We need to be about our Master's business. Let us submit ourselves to Him. If we have become slack in prayer, let us turn again toward the Lord. If we have become slack in study, let us revive the habit of daily study – touching base, so to speak, every day. This is where we need to be. We must be attentive to the way the Holy Spirit works in us, transforming us day by day through the renewing of our minds — a process we facilitate by a daily habit of prayer and study.

"Before David was born, his destiny was designed by God. His great grandparents were Boaz and Ruth, and his grandfather was Obed whose son was Jesse, David's father. David spent the beginning of his life caring for his father's sheep and spending many days and nights alone with God. This was the beginning of David's destiny, and it would seem to him that this was all there was in his life. I look at the life of David; he didn't start out in the position of a King, but David had to go through several avenues of training. Training qualifies and equips you for a position that one (or even God) may feel as if you are designed for. David began his training for Kingship by serving as a shepherd. Now according to Merriam-Webster dictionary, a shepherd is a person whose job is to take care of the sheep. David had to not only care for sheep, but he had to fight for the sheep which helped to develop David's fighting skills. There was this Philistine that was making a lot of noise around town, and he had people in an uproar. Regardless of what each opponent of the Philistine had, it was not enough to defeat this giant. But here comes David, who had been in training. Now to Saul and others, David didn't seem like a match to this Philistine, and I could imagine them probably laughing at David, saying, Now who do he really think that he is? That was an opportunity for David to disclose the victories he had obtained through his training. In 1 Samuel 17:34-37 David states:

And David said unto Saul, Thy servant kept his father's sheep, and there came a lion, and a bear, and took a lamb out of the flock: And I went out after him, and smote him, and delivered it out of his mouth: and when he arose against me, I caught him by his beard and smote him, and slew him. Thy servant slew both the lion and the bear: and this uncircumcised Philistine shall be as one of them, seeing he hath defied the armies of the living God. David said moreover, The Lord, that delivered me out of the paw of the lion, and out of the paw of the lion, and out of the paw of the bear, he will deliver me out of the hand of this Philistine: And Saul said unto David, Go, and the Lord be with thee" (www.flowerheaven.wordpress.com).

David was the youngest of Jesse's eight sons. He cared for his father's sheep. He was mocked by his brothers for being a shepherd, and despite their mockery, he killed Goliath the giant. He had killed the lion and the bear defending the sheep, now it was time to kill a giant named Goliath, defending a nation. It seemed so farfetched that this shepherd boy would become a king with all the persecution that was generated against him by the ruling king Saul. It was what was hidden inside David that really counted. Only God knew, the empowerment of the anointing by the hand of Samuel would bring to light the inward work that was of God. When people looked at David, they only saw a shepherd boy, not a king. But when God looked at David, He saw the destiny He purposed for him. He saw a warrior king emerging who would bring a nation together.

Returning from a great slaughter of the Philistines, David and Saul were greeted by the handmaidens of the cities who sang encouragement. Their encouragement was Saul's discouragement because they gave greater praise to David than to Saul. Jealousy began to fester in Saul's heart, and David's life was in danger. He became a fugitive. For many years, with a call on his life to be king, he was hunted as a common criminal by Saul and his armies. David did nothing to offend Saul, "He behaved wisely in all his ways and the Lord was with him" (I Samuel 18:14). Yet in spite of Saul's attempts to kill David, he never retaliated or looked for revenge. What kept David sane was, he would not touch God's anointed (Psalm 105:15). There were times when David had the advantage over Saul, yet he would not harm or kill him. David eventually became king after Saul died, having killed himself after receiving a fatal wound during the battle against the Philistines. David reigned over Judah seven years and six months. He reigned in Jerusalem thirty-three years over all of Israel and Judah (II Samuel 5:5). He had quite a life running from Saul; it didn't go to waste. Rather, it prepared him for the time when he would be king. David was known in the courts of the Lord, in that heavenly realm as, "a man after His own heart" (1 Samuel 13:14). This is proof that in order to reach a level of greatness you must go through your training.

Taking a break from David, and looking at my own life, I went through a lot of things (such as the death of my only son) that I didn't think was right. I looked at all those people around me that didn't walk with God whole-heartedly. I looked at people that treated their children as if they were a curse instead of a blessing. I watched those people, and I could have easily questioned God and said, "God, why not them?' Corey had two parents that not only loved him, but most importantly loved God. But now I understand that was a part of my life that I had to go through for my training. God knew (way before I did) that I would be a Pastor of a church, Empowering Tabernacle House of Prayer Outreach Ministry Apostolic Faith that would have over 200 people on the role. He knew that I would be hurt during my Pastoral assignment.

45

He knew that I would be disliked for no reason at all. God knew that people were going to turn their back on me. God wanted to make sure, I, Phillip Maurice Jackson, could deal with a lot and what better way to be trained in that area than by losing my only son. So, while in ministry, when people walked away, I was hurt but only to a certain extent. Why, because I had been trained in that area, and I thank God that I became victorious. Also, through my years of Pastoring, I have come across many people that have lost loved ones, and for them, their life was over. I even pastor a couple whose daughter was brutally killed. During those times of counseling, I began to see again why it was necessary for me and my wife to go through what we went through. Now this is not to say that in order to be fully qualified as a Pastor you must lose a child; this is only to say that this is the cup that my wife and I had to drink. And when those broken people came in our presence (my wife and I) we could boldly tell them God is a comforter, how God is able to uphold you in times of distress. We could so easily give those words of encouragement because God had been all of that and more to us during our times of suffering. Then we could go on to say that if God did it for us, He can do it for you. That season of our life was for our training.

Now, David went on to conquer Goliath with a sling and a stone. He was victorious in that area but was not yet actually named as the "King". The women even began to play and sing a song about his victory, 1 Samuel 18: 7, "And the women answered one another as they played, and said, Saul hath slain his thousands, and David his ten thousands". That phrase would have been enough for David to think that his training was over, and he was ready to be king. Just think about some minor victories that we have accomplished in the ministry. With the victory and the people's compliments, some of us thought we were ready to start our own church with our training incomplete. But David patiently continued in his training, and he began to serve faithfully unto Saul. This was no easy task, because hatred had filled Saul's heart for David, and he made several attempts to actually kill David. What is so awesome about David's training in this particular area, David knew that Saul was making attempts on his life, but David would not turn an evil heart towards Saul. He had every opportunity to kill Saul and probably would have had a valid excuse, but David (knowing God's word) proclaimed, "Don't destroy him! Who can lay a hand on the Lord's anointed and be guiltless?" (1 Samuel 26:9). Many people could not endure this type of treatment. Plenty of people cry out to God to humble them, and I can imagine God saying "Okay". So, He'll put them on a job with a manager that is doing everything to destroy them (Saul). Before they go through that type of training, they will quit, but not before telling that manager how they feel. Training was over, and he was ready to be king. Well, the answer is quite simple, they aborted their training. But David endured this treatment as a good soldier, and when God saw fit to kill Saul, then David was made King. His training had become complete. He went from being known only as Jesse's son, to being just a shepherd, to being known as the one who defeated Goliath, to being known as Saul's faithful servant, to ultimately being known for being a mighty King who will forever be known as a man after God's own heart. His training brought forth his transition.

In continuing with our transition to greatness, I'm reminded of the story of Cain and Abel. Looking at their lives, we learn a lot about the pain of rejection and how it can have a negative impact on us if we allow anger and bitterness to set in. After Adam and Eve ate the fruit that God told them not to eat, they had to move out of the beautiful Garden of Eden. Their lives were harder now because they had chosen to disobey God. "Adam and Eve had a baby, and they called him Cain. His mother said, "I have gotten a man from the Lord" (www.landerroark.wordpress.com). Perhaps she thought he would be the one who God promised would defeat Satan. Even if she didn't, she certainly had high hopes for her firstborn son. Then Adam and Eve had another baby boy. He was named Abel. Cain and Abel were different in many ways. Cain grew up to be a farmer. Abel raised sheep. More important, their attitude toward God was different. Abel gave an offering to God, and it was

49

the best he had. Abel believed and trusted God (Hebrews 11:4). Cain also gave an offering to God, but the Bible says God was not happy with it. Cain got very angry. Perhaps he felt it was unfair. Maybe he was jealous that God was happy with Abel. But God cared about Cain, too. He asked Cain, "Why are you angry?" God told Cain that if he did the right things, God would be happy with him. But if not, he was in danger of sin. Just as when Satan talked Cain's parents into sinning, sin was waiting to pounce on Cain. God told him to rule over these bad attitudes. But Cain didn't listen. He got angrier and convinced himself he was right.

Sin can lead us to do things we do not plan to do. The results of our sinful thoughts and actions may be far worse than we ever intended. Cain was so mad that he murdered his brother! Cain killed Abel because Cain's "works were evil and his brother's righteous" (1 John 3:12). He didn't like being shown up by his younger brother. Satan is a hater, and Cain chose to hate, too. So, when they were alone in the field, Cain killed Abel. Cain thought no one had seen him do it. But Cain should have known that he couldn't hide from God. God knew what happened, but he gave Cain the chance to admit it. God asked Cain, "Where is Abel your brother"? Cain said, "I do not know. Am I my brother's keeper"? But Cain lied. He knew exactly where Abel's body was. And he knew that we all should do our best to take care of our brothers. We can't control our brothers and sisters, but we shouldn't do anything to hurt them. We should help and care for them. In that way we, are our brother's keeper.

God knew exactly what Cain had done. He knew Cain was lying. It was as if Abel's shed blood was crying out to God that a terrible murder occurred. Cain's final punishment would be to die. But before that, God told Cain about the curses he would face. The ground wouldn't grow as much food for him, and he would have to work harder. He would have to move around and worry that others would try to kill him. Cain complained that the punishment was too much. He did not say he was sorry. He did not admit that he had done a terrible thing. But God did not want other people to take revenge on Cain.

He put a mark on Cain to remind people not to kill him. Cain picked the road that leads to death. He chose to be selfish. He chose to trust in himself instead of God. He chose to think about his hurt pride. The Bible calls this the way of Cain (Jude 1:11). The story of Cain provides an example of the wrong response to rejection. Through this study, we learn not only what happens in a typical rejection scenario, but also what we can do to avoid the potential harm it can cause when it's not put in check. We must remember that when we get mad, sin is waiting to pounce on us too. We must remember that hating others is like murder (1 John 3:15). We must ask God to help us rule over ourselves and sin. We must care for our brothers and sisters and not respond like Cain did. Jesus is our perfect example of how to 'stay right when you feel like you've been done wrong'.

Two more individuals I love to read about in their training is Elisha with Elijah. Elisha was the faithful disciple and successor of the prophet Elijah. He had followed his master from the moment they met, when Elisha was a young man, plowing his father's field near the ancient town of Abel-mecholah in northern Israel. Elisha saw his master disappear in a fiery chariot, going up to Heaven, without dying first. At that moment, Elisha cried: "My father, my father, the chariot of Israel...!" and rent his clothes. He knew then that he was to carry on the great work of Elijah, to spread the knowledge of God, to bring relief and blessing to his people, and teach them to be kind and charitable. Elisha picked up the mantle which Elijah had cast off when he went up to heaven. He felt the spirit of Elijah within him, and when he had to cross the Jordan to return home, he waved Elijah's mantle against the water, and they parted suddenly and made a way for the divine prophet to cross the Jordan on its dry bed.

In Jericho, the band of young prophets saw Elisha make his miraculous crossing of the Jordan alone. They knew Elijah disappeared, and they hailed Elisha as their leader and master. Soon, Elisha was again to prove his divine powers. The people of Jericho came to him to complain of the bad water in the vicinity which caused disease to man and beast and laid the whole land waste and barren. Elisha was ready to prove God's great kindness in a miraculous way. "He requested a new cruse with salt. This he took to the nearest spring and there cast the salt into the water" (www.lifeissues.net). To the assembled people he proclaimed in God's name that the water would now be cured, and would no longer cause death, nor make the land barren. As the people drank of the sweet, pure and wholesome water, they praised God and blessed the great prophet. Elisha's name grew far and wide. Having left Jericho in the company of his disciples, the younger prophets, Elisha was approaching the town of Beth-el. Instead of greeting the prophet and his disciples with respect and honor, some young men of Beth-el came out to mock the prophet and shout abusive words in his direction. The reason for their disgraceful behavior was their great selfishness. Until Elisha cured the water in the vicinity, they had a profitable business. They used to bring water from afar and get high prices for it from the local inhabitants. But since Elisha cured the water, they lost this business, and therefore hated the prophet. Seeing that these people had no fear of God, and no respect for the prophet, or any consideration for their fellowmen, Elisha cursed them, and their punishment came swiftly. Ferocious bears suddenly appeared from the woods and charged into the mocking crowd. Forty-two young men were left slain, and the rest fled in terror.

We, as Christians, must know that there is a purpose in our pain. We all will say that we want to be great in the eyesight of God, but the key to that position is our training. We must know that every trial and tribulation that we go through is for our making. So what I was raped as a child, so what I come from a dysfunctional family, and so what if many thought there wasn't much to me. You have to learn to be so thankful for those dark places because they proved to be your training for what God really has in store you. This is your path from being the least to the greatest. It's in your training!

CHAPTER 3

BEING TRANSLATED: THE LIFE OF ENOCH

Enoch (the son of Jared), holds a rare distinction in the Bible: He did not die. Instead, God "took him away". Scripture does not reveal much about this remarkable man. We find his story in Genesis 5, in a long list of the descendants of Adam. Only a short sentence, "Enoch walked faithfully with God," in Genesis 5:22 and repeated in Genesis 5:24 reveals why he was so special to his Creator. In this wicked period before the Flood, most men did *not* walk faithfully with God. They walked their own path, the crooked way of sin. Enoch did not keep silent about the sin around him. Jude says Enoch prophesied about those evil people: *"See, the Lord is coming with thousands upon thousands of his holy ones to judge everyone, and to convict all of them of all the ungodly acts they have committed in their ungodliness, and of all the defiant words ungodly sinners have spoken against him"*(Jude 1:14-15, NIV). Enoch walked in faith the 365 years of his life, and that made all the difference. No matter what happened, he trusted God. He obeyed God. God loved Enoch so much that He spared him the experience of death. Hebrews 11, that great Faith Hall of Fame passage, says Enoch's faith pleased God: *For before he was taken, he was commended as one who pleased God. And without faith it is impossible to please God, because anyone who comes to Him must believe that He exists and that He rewards those who earnestly seek Him* (Hebrews 11:5-6, NIV). What happened to Enoch? The Bible gives few details, other than to say: *"then he was no more, because God took him away"* (Genesis 5:24, NIV). Only one other person in Scripture was honored this way: the prophet Elijah. God took that faithful servant to heaven in a whirlwind (2 Kings 2:11). Enoch's great-grandson, Noah, also "walked faithfully with God" (Genesis 6:9). Because of his righteousness, only Noah and his family were spared in the Great Flood. And Enoch walked with God: and he was not; for God took him (Genesis 5:24).Enoch is one of the few excellent men mentioned in the Bible, of whom nothing bad is recorded. Abraham is described as the father of the faithful; and yet there are instances on record in which his mighty faith gave way. Whoever thinks of the flaws on the face of beauty? Whoever thinks of the spots which deface the sun? They exist, you may find them by minute observation; but they do not make a deep impression upon your mind. Thus the character of Enoch, in the midst of a wicked and perverse generation, seemed to be one mass of light, in which there was no darkness at all. Enoch is one of these men who owe their immortality to the brightness of their characters. His could be considered, a simple record of a glorious life. What does a glorious life consist of? "The poet thinks it a glorious thing to produce burning thoughts, to master the powers of language, to command brilliant imagery; to revel in imagination through the ethereal regions of the lovely, the grand, the eternal; and then descend from those lofty heights to the lowly regions of real life, to enlighten its gloom, to soothe its sorrows, to strengthen its hopes" (www.biblehub.com).

The orator thinks it a glorious thing to rivet the attention of assembled multitudes. The warrior thinks it a glorious thing to be entrusted with the command of a powerful army. Here is a simple record of a glorious life; let us now endeavor to analyze it. The words point to, a life of absolute devotedness. It is not a selfish existence, but an existence linked to another existence, subordinate to another existence, devoted to another existence. "With God." A life of steady progress. This is clearly suggested by the term walking. Man is never more dignified than when he walks with a regular, firm, steady step; it is then that he looks every inch the lord of creation; you wonder not those other creatures should submit to his sway. But let him loiter about as if he had nothing to do, or let him run as if he were pursued, and he falls at once in your estimation. There is a touch of manliness about the very act of walking, which indicates a definite purpose, a reasonable aim, a complete mastery over oneself. You have only to conceive of a man walking and a man running, and compare these two conceptions together, in order to be impressed with the superiority of the one over the other. But the expression employed here has a wider meaning than this. "Enoch walked with God." This indicates progress. It is progress in knowledge, progress in holiness, progress in good works. It is an upward struggle, a Heavenward course, a climbing up to the mount of God. Now, the blessed companionship of Enoch with God, which was a type of all true companionship, implied faith in God. Enoch's companionship also implied a certain degree of familiarity with God. Just think of it. God's friend must become a God-like character. The moon which is bathed in the transforming light of the sun, becomes itself a luminous body, and lightens up the somber blackness of the night with its pale, beautiful, silvery rays. And so, the man who walks in the light of God's countenance must necessarily catch some of the glory and reflect it upon the world around him. Besides this, God's friend needs fear no enemy. Enoch was a loyal follower of God – he was faithful to God and obedient. He told the truth despite opposition and ridicule. Thus, it's recorded, that this man of excellence had a glorious end. "And he was not, for

God took him." A good man is never lost; long after his body has moldered in the dust, the influence of his holy example will remain, will remain as a mighty power; a power which will not diminish, but grow with the flight of ages. Enoch and the other Old Testament heroes mentioned in the Faith Hall of Fame walked in faith, in the hope of a future Messiah (Genesis5:24). That Messiah has been revealed to us in the gospels as Jesus Christ. When we trust Christ as Savior and walk with God, as Enoch did, we will die physically, but will be resurrected to eternal life. Now faith is the assurance (the confirmation, the title deed) of the things we hope for, being the proof of things, we do not see *and* the conviction of their reality. Through their faith, the people in days of old earned a good reputation. By faith we understand that the entire universe was formed at God's command, and that what we now see did not come from anything that can be seen (Hebrews11:1).

> "It was by faith that Enoch was taken up to heaven without dying… For before he was taken up, he was known as a person who pleased God. And it is impossible to please God without faith. Anyone who

wants to come to him must believe that God exists and that he rewards those who sincerely seek him" (www.biblehub.com).

Some sectors tend to believe that heaven can only be explored after death. I believe differently, and so I behave differently. Paul talks about being taken up to the third heaven. There are multiple verses where Jesus "looked up to heaven" that actually means more literally, he looked into Heaven (like, pop your head through the clouds and look around). Then, right here with Enoch, we see an Old Testament picture of somebody being taken to Heaven without dying. So, the testimonies in the bible and in life are there not just to show you what happened once and never again, but to set a precedence for the things that God wants to do. It's the whole, "the increase of his government and of peace there shall be no end" (Isaiah 9:7) "greater works than these will you do things" (John 14:12). The quicker people can get over the mindset that God did the grand finale during bible days, and has switched to lighting off sparklers ever since, the more of an opportunity they will have of actually beginning to explore the furthest reaches of their potential here on earth. I have said it before, and I will say it again: the limitations of what people can explore here on earth are set by man much more than they are set by God.

CHAPTER 4

THE PRODIGAL SON

The Parable of the Prodigal Son is found in Luke chapter 15, verses 11-32. The main character in the parable, the forgiving father, whose character remains constant throughout the story, is a picture of God. In telling the story, Jesus identifies Himself with God in His loving attitude to the lost. The younger son symbolizes the lost (the tax collectors and sinners of that day, Luke 15:1), and the elder brother represents the self-righteous (the Pharisees and teachers of the law of that day, Luke 15:2). The major theme of this parable seems not to be so much the conversion of the sinner, as in the previous two parables of Luke 15, but rather the restoration of a believer into fellowship with the Father. In the first two parables, the owner went out to look for what was lost (Luke 15:1-10), whereas in this story, the father waits and watches eagerly for his son's return. We see a progression through the three parables from the relationship of one in a hundred (Luke 15:1-7), to one in ten (Luke 15:8-10), to one in one (Luke 15:11-32), demonstrating God's love for each individual and His personal attentiveness towards all humanity. We see in this story the graciousness of the father overshadowing the sinfulness of the son, as it is the memory of the father's goodness that brings the prodigal son to repentance (Romans 2:4).

We will begin unfolding the meaning of this parable at verse 12, in which the younger son asks his father for his share of his estate, which would have been half of what his older brother would receive; in other words, one-third for the younger, two-thirds for the older (Deuteronomy 21:17). Though it was perfectly within his right to ask, it was not a loving thing to do, as it implied that he wished his father dead. Instead of rebuking his son, the father patiently grants him his request. This is a picture of God letting a sinner go his own way (Deuteronomy 30:19). We all possess this foolish ambition to be independent, which is at the root of the sinner persisting in his sin (Genesis 3:6; Romans 1:28). A sinful state is a departure and distance from God (Romans 1:21). A sinful state is also a state of constant discontent. Luke 12:15 says, "Watch out! Be on your guard against all kinds of greed; a man's life does not consist in the abundance of his possessions." This son learned the hard way that covetousness leads to a life of dissatisfaction and disappointment. He also learned that the most valuable things in life are the things you cannot buy or replace.

In Luke 15:13, we read that he travels to a distant country. It is evident from his previous actions that he had already made that journey in his heart, and the physical departure was a display of his willful disobedience to all the goodness his father had offered (Proverbs 27:19; Matthew 6:21; 12:34). In the process, he squanders all his father had worked so hard for on selfish, shallow fulfillment, losing everything. His financial disaster is followed by a natural disaster in the form of a famine, which he failed to plan for (Genesis 41:33-36). At this point he sells himself into physical slavery to a Gentile and finds himself feeding pigs, a detestable job to the Jewish people (Leviticus 11:7; Deuteronomy 14:8;

Isaiah 65:4; 66:17). Needless to say, he must have been incredibly desperate at that point to willingly enter into such a loathsome position. And what an irony that his choices led him to a position in which he had no choice but to work, and for a stranger at that, doing the very things he refused to do for his father. To top it off, he apparently was paid so little that he longed to eat the pig's food. Just when he must have thought life could not get any worse, he could not even find mercy among the people. Apparently, once his wealth was gone, so were his friends. The text clearly says, "No one gave him anything" (Luke 15:16). Even these unclean animals seemed to be better off than he was at this point. This is a picture of the state of the lost sinner or a rebellious Christian who has returned to a life of slavery to sin (2 Peter 2:19-21). It is a picture of what sin really does in a person's life when he rejects the Father's will (Hebrews 12:1; Acts 8:23). "Sin always promises more than it gives, takes you further than you wanted to go, and leaves you worse off than you were before". Sin promises freedom but brings slavery (John 8:34).

The son begins to reflect on his condition and realizes that even his father's servants had it better than he. His painful circumstances help him to see his father in a new light and bring him hope (Psalm 147:11; Isaiah 40:30-31; Romans 8:24-25; 1 Timothy 4:10). This is reflective of the sinner when he/she discovers the destitute condition of his life because of sin. It is a realization that, apart from God, there is no hope (Ephesians 2:12; 2 Timothy 2:25-26). This is when a repentant sinner "comes to his senses" and longs to return to the state of fellowship with God which was lost when Adam sinned (Genesis 3:8). The son devises a plan of action. Though at a quick glance it may seem that he may not be truly repentant, but rather motivated by his hunger, a more thorough study of the text gives new insights. He is willing to give up his rights as his father's son and take on the position of his servant. We can only speculate on this point, but he may even have been willing to repay what he had lost (Luke 19:8; Leviticus 6:4-5). Regardless of the motivation, it demonstrates a true humility and true repentance, not based on what he said but on what he was willing to do and eventually acted upon (Acts 26:20). He realizes he had no right to claim a blessing upon return to his father's household, nor did he have anything to offer, except a life of service, in repentance of his previous actions. With that, he was prepared to fall at his father's feet and hope for forgiveness and mercy. This is exactly what conversion is all about: ending a life of slavery to sin through confession to the Father and faith in Jesus Christ and becoming a slave to righteousness, offering one's body as a living sacrifice (1 John 1:9; Romans 6:6-18; 12:1).

Jesus portrays the father as waiting for his son, perhaps daily searching the distant road, hoping for his appearance. The father notices him while he was still a long way off. The father's compassion assumes some knowledge of the son's pitiful state, possibly from reports sent home. During that time, it was not the custom of men to run, yet the father runs to greet his son (Luke 15:20). Why would he break convention for this wayward child who had sinned against him? The obvious answer is because he loved him and was eager to show him that love and restore the relationship. When the father reaches his son, not only does he throw his arms around him, but he also greets him with a kiss of love (1 Peter 5:14). He is so filled with joy at his son's return that he does not even let him finish his confession, nor does he question or lecture him. Instead, he unconditionally forgives him and accepts him back into fellowship. The father, running to his son, greeting him with a kiss and ordering the celebration, is a picture of how our Heavenly Father feels towards sinners who repent. God greatly loves us, patiently waits for us to repent so He can show us His great mercy, because He does not want any to perish nor escape as though by the fire (Ephesians 2:1-10; 2 Peter 3:9; 1 Corinthians 3:15).

This prodigal son was satisfied to return home as a slave, but to his surprise and delight is restored back into the full privilege of being his father's son. He had been transformed from a state of destitution to complete restoration. That is what God's grace does for a repentant sinner (Psalm 40:2; 103:4). Not only are we forgiven, but we receive a spirit of sonship as His children, heirs of God and co-heirs with Christ, of His incomparable riches (Romans 8:16-17; Ephesians 1:18-19). The father then orders the servants to bring the best robe, no doubt one of his own (a sign of dignity and honor, proof of the prodigal's acceptance back into the family), a ring for the son's hand (a sign of authority and sonship) and sandals for his feet (a sign of not being a servant, as servants did not wear shoes – or, for that matter, rings or expensive clothing, (Luke 15:22). All these things represent what we receive in Christ upon salvation: the robe of the Redeemer's righteousness (Isaiah 61:10), the privilege of partaking of the Spirit of adoption (Ephesians 1:5), and feet fitted with the readiness that comes from the gospel of peace, prepared to walk in the ways of holiness (Ephesians 6:15). A fattened calf is prepared, and a party is held (notice that blood was shed as atonement for sin (Hebrews 9:22). Fatted calves in those times were saved for special occasions such as the Day of Atonement (Leviticus 23:26-32). This was not just any party; it was a rare and complete celebration. Had the boy been dealt with according to the Law, there would have been a funeral, not a celebration.

> "The Lord does not treat us as our sins deserve or repay us according to our iniquities. For as high as the heavens are above the earth, so great is his love for those who fear him; as far as the east is from the west, so far has he removed our transgressions from us. As a father has compassion on his children, so the Lord has compassion on those who fear him" (Psalm 103:10-13).

Instead of condemnation, there is rejoicing for a son who had been dead but now is alive, who once was lost but now is found (Romans 8:1; John 5:24). Note the parallel between "dead" and "alive" and "lost" and "found" – terms that also apply to one's state before and after conversion to Christ (Ephesians 2:1-5). This is a picture of what occurs in heaven over one repentant sinner (Luke 15: 7, 10).

Now to the final and tragic character in the Parable of the Prodigal Son, the oldest son, who, once again, illustrates the Pharisees and the scribes. Outwardly they lived blameless lives, but inwardly their attitudes were abominable (Matthew 23:25-28). This was true of the older son who worked hard, obeyed his father, and brought no disgrace to his family or townspeople. It is obvious by his words and actions, upon his brothers return, that he is not showing love for his father or brother. One of the duties of the eldest son would have included reconciliation between the father and his son. He would have been the host at the feast to celebrate his brother's return. Yet he remains in the field instead of in the house where he should have been. This act alone would have brought public disgrace upon the father. Still, the father, with great patience, goes to his angry and hurting son. He does not rebuke him as his actions and disrespectful address of his father warrant (vs.29, "Look," he says, instead of addressing him as "father" or "my lord"), nor does his compassion cease as he listens to his complaints and criticisms. The boy appeals to his father's righteousness by proudly proclaiming his own self-righteousness in comparison to his brother's sinfulness (Matthew 7:3-5). By saying, "This son of yours," the older brother avoids acknowledging that the prodigal is his own brother (Luke 15:30). Just like the Pharisees, the older brother was defining sin by outward actions, not inward

attitudes (Luke 18:9-14). In essence, the older brother is

saying that he was the one worthy of the celebration, and

his father had been ungrateful for all his work. Now the

one who had squandered his wealth was getting what he,

the older son, deserved. The father tenderly addresses

his oldest as "my son" (Luke 15:31) and corrects the error

in his thinking by referring to the prodigal son as "this

brother of yours" (Luke 15:32). The father's response,

"We had to celebrate," suggests that the elder brother

should have joined in the celebration, as there seems to

be a sense of urgency in not postponing the celebration

of the brother's return.

The older brother's focus was on himself, and as a

result there is no joy in his brother's arrival home. He is

so consumed with issues of justice and equity that he

fails to see the value of his brother's repentance and

return.

> He fails to realize that "anyone who claims
> to be in the light, but hates his brother, is still in the
> darkness. Whoever loves his brother lives in the
> light, and there is nothing in him to make him
> stumble. But whoever hates his brother is in the

darkness; he does not know where he is going, because the darkness has blinded him" (1 John 2:9-11).

The older brother allows anger to take root in his heart to the point that he is unable to show compassion towards his brother, and, for that matter he is unable to forgive the perceived sin of his father against him (Genesis 4:5-8). He prefers to nurse his anger rather than enjoy fellowship with his father, brother and the community. He chooses suffering and isolation over restoration and reconciliation (Matthew 5:24, 6:14-15). He sees his brother's return as a threat to his own inheritance. After all, why should he have to share his portion with a brother who has squandered his? And why hadn't his father rejoiced in his presence through his faithful years of service? The wise father seeks to bring restoration by pointing out that all he has is and has always been available for the asking to his obedient son, as it was his portion of the inheritance since the time of the allotment. The older son never utilized the blessings at his disposal (Galatians 5:22; 2 Peter 1:5-8). This is similar to the Pharisees with their religion of good works.

They hoped to earn blessings from God and in their obedience merit eternal life (Romans 9:31-33; 10:3). They failed to understand the grace of God and failed to comprehend the meaning of forgiveness. It was, therefore, not what they did that became a stumbling block to their growth but rather what they did not do which alienated them from God (Matthew 23:23-24, Romans 10:4). They were irate when Jesus was receiving and forgiving "unholy" people, failing to see their own need for a Savior. We do not know how this story ended for the oldest son, but we do know that the Pharisees continued to oppose Jesus and separate themselves from His followers. Despite the father's pleading for them to "come in," they refused and were the ones who instigated the arrest and crucifixion of Jesus Christ (Matthew 26:59). A tragic ending to a story filled with such hope, mercy, joy, and forgiveness. The picture of the father receiving the son back into relationship is a picture of how we should respond to repentant sinners as well (1 John 4:20-21; Luke 17:3; Galatians 6:1; James 5:19-20). "All have sinned and fall short of the glory of

God" (Romans 3:23). We are included in that "all," and we must remember that "all our righteous acts are like filthy rags" apart from Christ (Isaiah 64:6; John 15:1-6). It is only by God's grace that we are saved, not by works that we may boast of (Ephesians 2:9; Romans 9:16; Psalm 51:5).

We need God's Assistance. And God's Assistant is Jesus. The devil is attacking all Believers and we need His Assistance in these last and evil days. Survive simply means to remain living. Though they slay you, you can remain alive. You can live and stand by the Blood of Jesus. Jesus is a Good Assistance, and the Word of God is your help; the 66 Books of the Bible. No more are you a slave unto the world. Now you are in sonship with Jesus Christ. How bad do you want it? I want the world to know that serving the Lord will pay off. If you don't believe that, then why do you come to church? Jesus don't need any workers, He need worshippers. God has all you need – if you need joy – He's got it! Your tribulations shouldn't make you faint, but it should make you glorify God. God can numb you;

He can give you a tranquilizer and mold you into the man or woman He would have you to be. Don't look at anyone else and don't pass judgment. Allow God to work on you. I thank God for being humble. The church has got to show the unchurched how to live. Those who are great among you, let them become a servant. Ephesians 3:16 says, "I pray that out of His glorious riches He may strengthen you with power through His Spirit in your inner being". It takes Jesus' Spirit to strengthen you in your mortal body. Yes, we need His Deliverance. For He is our shield – our very Present Help in the time of trouble. Therefore, we should always, give God all the Honor, Praise, and Glory that is due to Him. Our help is here, and His name is Jesus. That is the core message of the Parable of the Prodigal Son.

CHAPTER 5

STAYING FOCUSED DURING THE WAIT

There is one thing that people in our generation hate to do, and that is to wait. And why should we? We can go to the World Wide Web search for answers to our questions rather than wait for them. We can order and pay for shoes online rather than suffering the long weekend lines at the retail store. We can even book reservations to our favorite restaurants ahead of time rather than waiting. Our perspective on waiting is perhaps one of the stronger ways our society is out of step with the biblical worldview. Don't get me wrong, I'm not saying that waiting was any easier for our forefathers, but they were more at peace with it, and more ready to see its goodness and potential. In the Old Testament, the psalmist celebrates waiting patiently for the Lord (Psalm 40:1), and Isaiah promises that those "who wait for the Lord shall renew their strength; they shall mount up with wings like eagles; they shall run and not be weary; they shall walk and not faint" (Isaiah 40:31). Waiting on God is a regular refrain in the life of faith. It is an expression of the healthy heart's desire: "O Lord, we wait for you; your name and remembrance are the desire of our soul" (Isaiah 26:8). And it is an echo of the unparalleled power and grace of God, "who acts for those who wait for him" (Isaiah 64:4). Waiting centuries and centuries for the Messiah, you would think the waiting would be over once Jesus had come. But even now in the church age, we find ourselves waiting as much as ever; called to live in the shadow of His return. We "wait for the revealing of our Lord Jesus Christ" (1 Corinthians 1:7); we are a people "waiting for our blessed hope, the appearing of the glory of our great God and Savior Jesus Christ" (Titus 2:13). The church is that community which has "turned to God from idols to serve the living and true God, and to wait for His Son from Heaven" (1 Thessalonians 1:9-10), knowing that when He appears, He comes "to save those who are eagerly waiting for Him" (Hebrews 9:28). The church has endured two millennia of extended waiting. We "groan inwardly as we wait eagerly for adoption as sons, the redemption of our bodies" (Romans 8:23), and we aim to live in "holiness and godliness, waiting for and hastening the coming of the day of God . . . waiting for new heavens and a new earth in which righteousness dwells" (2 Peter 3:11–13). And as we bide our time on this side, we "keep ourselves in the love of God" by "waiting for the mercy of our Lord Jesus Christ that leads to eternal life" (Jude 21).

Some days, it is hard to be patient. When we bring our concerns to the Lord over and over again, we grow tired of waiting. After a while, it begins to feel like our prayers are falling on deaf ears. Often our desire is to take control of the situation(s) and handle it ourselves; it is our fleshly reaction to the silence. But Galatians 5 lists patience as one of the fruits of the Holy Spirit. Therefore, we must confess our desire to rule our lives and take matters into our own hands. We must ask the Spirit to fill us, empower us and direct us as we continue to wait patiently on the Lord. Even still, this doesn't mean your circumstances will automatically. Having prayed fervently about whatever issue you're facing too many times to count, can easily deplete your bank of patience. On these days, let these reminders on the nature of patience be an

encouragement to you as you continue to wait.

The New Bible Dictionary defines patience as "a God-given restraint in the face of opposition or oppression". Patience is only needed when there is a reason not to wait. It is only necessary in the face of opposition. This is why seeking patience is in many instances a battle. As Christians, the promise we have to lean on, is that patience is God-given restraint. The Lord is the one Who provides us with spiritual armor to go into battle. We often think of patience as mere endurance, but such logic is faulty. We are not exercising restraint in our own strength. In truth, the only thing we have to do is trust that God will provide the strength for us to hold on, and then act accordingly to our faith in that promise. How is this strength given to us? We receive this strength by being filled with the Holy Spirit. As Christians, we know that the ultimate source of patience lives within us. Our role is to trust that the Holy Spirit does reside within us, and ask Him for strength to persevere in whatever situation we find ourselves in. This is a provision we can claim by faith as taught to us in Romans 5:1-5. Patience as listed in Galatians 5 is often called longsuffering. "The original Greek word is makrothumio, meaning "long temper". We are be patient and longsuffering; have a slow temper towards ourselves and others. This spiritual posture calls for Grace. It is Grace that compels us to trust God; Grace that we can extend to others when they hurt us, and Grace to forgive ourselves when we stumble and fall. The experience of waiting on God reminds us that our reality as Christians is not within our apparent circumstances, but rather in the truth of Christ's love and life within us. This gives us hope, as Romans 8:28 assures us that "we know that in all things God works for the good of those who love Him, who have been called according to His purpose". It is not in our abilities to know the time or way in which God will work things out. Ecclesiastes 3:11 and Isaiah 55:8-9 are great reminders that these rest solely in the domain of God's knowledge. Our role is to trust the promise of Philippians 1:6 and wait with hope as God brings about to completion the good work He began in each of our lives. God allows us to access Divine restraint, but it is our choice to accept it and act in willful obedience. Adam and Eve were given free will in the Garden of Eden. They were given many privileges and provisions in the garden so they wouldn't need to partake of the forbidden fruit. However, they chose not to exercise restraint and instead disobeyed God's command. When we use God-given restraint to wait on His timing, we renounce their fallen actions and step out in obedience towards God. Rest assured, there is purpose in the process. Take a look at Hebrews 12:2. Waiting on God forces us to look to Him. It casts our eyes rightly to Christ as the Source of our faith and the assurance of our Salvation. It reminds us that Jesus' life and death is the reason we can be filled with and empowered by the Holy Spirit. Trials and tribulations cause us to persevere by deepening our knowledge of God and relying on Him more than anyone else. As James 1:2-4 tells us it is here that a mature and complete faith is grown. Standing patiently when we wait on the Lord does not mean being stuck at a standstill. Consider Ephesians 6:11,13; which instructs us to "put on the full armor of God, so that when the day of evil comes, you may be able to stand your ground, and after you have done everything, to stand. Stand firm then". To stand grounded by remaining obedient to the Lord while waiting is not passive. Note that the word stand is repeated three times. Patience is an act of the will to stand firm and armored for the Kingdom of God, and is rewarded richly by

Him. Revelation 3:10-11 speaks of God's care for those who persevere through the battle. Whether we feel we lack patience to wait on God, or to continue to love those that may be hard to love, we do in actuality have access to all the patience we need.We can trust God to give us the strength to bear our circumstances and instead use the time of waiting to grow in intimacy with the Lord. While our natural inclination is to hate waiting, this period of uncertainty can actually be a time of great personal growth. The key to staying focused during 'the wait', is perseverance (thelife.com).

The testing of your faith develops perseverance" (James 1:3). We don't need perseverance for the quick solution(s). We need perseverance for the long haul; for the problems that just don't go away. "Have you been facing a trial in your life for 5, 10, or even 20 years? Both Paul and James have the answer for you. God's Power, is available to see you through. That's what perseverance is all about (www.biblicalcounselinginsights.com)!

Many Christians don't want to hear this, but God's word clearly states it – some problems are here to stay for a long time. The same power that is available for instant miracles, is the same power that will help us face the long-term problem situations. God's awesome power is available to help us develop perseverance as we face everyday trials. When those trials are someone else's problem and they 'dump garbage at our feet', we can't force that person to change. But we can use God's power to respond to the situation with Godly character. James offers more benefits as we face our problems over the long haul. "Perseverance must finish its work so that you may be mature and complete, not lacking anything." (James 1:4) We all want to be "mature and complete." But God, just give me your blessing! Let this be my path to spiritual maturity! But God's word is clear; the path to maturity is learning how to face our problems with His power. God promises He will never leave us or forsake us. (Deuteronomy 31:6) Our own decisions have taken us down paths filled with all kinds of problems. God's solution requires us to do more than face our problems. He also calls us to be His disciples – to follow Him. Some of our problems are the result of failing to follow Him. We went our own way and ended up in a big mess. Facing our problems in our own strength, using our own wisdom, can be the formula for disaster, not joy. Paul discovered the secret of joy in his life by learning to let God's power work through him in his times of weakness. Pure joy is yours if you will simply reach out and take it. With the strings God attaches, you'll be able to face trials of many kinds, and use His power to deal with them.

Everything that God allows to happen in your life is permitted for one great, eternal purpose: to conform and to mold your character to the image of Jesus Christ. It is for your growth and God's glory and it is a plan guaranteed to succeed. It will be completed when you get to Heaven. Since God intends to make you like Jesus, He is going to take you through the same experiences Jesus went through - including loneliness, temptation, stress, grief, criticism, abandonment, betrayal, rejection, hatred and many other kinds of problems. Why would God exempt us from what He allowed His own Son to experience? The Bible says Jesus "learned obedience through suffering" (Hebrews 5:8) and "was made perfect through suffering" (Hebrews 2:10). We grow the same way, and Jesus is our model. "We go through exactly what Christ goes through. If we go through the hard times with Him, then we're certainly going to go through the good times with Him" (Romans 8:17). Some mistakenly believe that God never wants Christians to suffer. But becoming like Jesus means serving, sacrificing, and suffering just as He did. The Bible repeatedly states that suffering is often the will of God for our lives. In fact, we sometimes suffer more because we are Christians. God tells us to consider this a privilege. "Anyone who wants to live all out for Christ is in for a lot of trouble; there's no getting around it" (2 Timothy 3:12). "God's goodness and grace doesn't mean you'll never be hurt, sad, or unhappy; and for some, it is greater than for others. God allows pain because He is more interested in your character than your comfort" (Lucado: 14). He wants to perfect you, not pamper you, and His goal for your life is holiness, not happiness. He always values the spiritual over the material, because that is what will last forever. The rewards of His character will be eternal. Sometimes God allows Satan to take away temporary comfort, as in the case of Job, to produce eternal character. Don't be surprised or complain of "unfairness" or become bitter by this. Realize it's all a part of the maturing process and an eternal goal you may not see until you see heaven.

God has a blueprint plan of our lives, written in the palm of His hand. "See, I have inscribed you on the palms of My hands; your walls are continually before Me." (Isaiah 49:16) The Bible says we do not have because we do not ask. Therefore, if we don't know God's direction in our lives, we simply ought to try asking Him for guidance. By prayerfully seeking direction, surrendering completely to Him, and listening attentively to His will (whatever it may be), what once seemed mysterious and unrecognizable will become amazingly clear. Suddenly, we will begin to see things we couldn't see before. "God our Heavenly Father, loving Counselor, peace-giving Friend, and gentle Shepherd is laden with gifts that will change our lives. However, we must be prayerfully attentive to the direction He has for us and to discern the path He has chosen from the one we have chosen for ourselves" (www.cbn.com). When we follow God's will and live according to His divine plan, our perspective shifts. Our vision expands and we begin to look at life not in terms of what we can do, but what God can do through us. We soon realize that nothing can distract, destroy, discourage, disappoint or defeat us when we follow God's direction. For instance, consider distractions. Isn't that when most of us get lost along the way? We start out to accomplish our purpose, then some other good thing comes along and before we know it, we've taken a left turn, landed just a few degrees off target, and lost the goal completely. But when we keep God's purpose in mind, we are empowered by the Spirit of God to accomplish it. "I submit that when you live according to God's plan, not only can nothing distract you, but also nothing can destroy you. Isn't that exciting? Jesus did not fear destruction because He was on target with His plan" (www.cbn.com). He knew what God had prepared for Him and He lived in the confidence and the courage of that understanding without discouragement. It is often easy to get discouraged. However, when we focus on God's direction as it is laid before us, we can overcome the urge to flee His plan. By doing so, we will not be disappointed and consequently, by living according to God's plan we will not be defeated.

I have learned in my Christian walk that the hardest thing for many Christians to do is to wait. If you tell them God is going to deliver them, God is going to set them free, or even if you say, God is getting ready to bless you like never before, they will get very excited. But when you say to them, you have to wait on it, it's like you have torn their hearts to pieces. It is imperative that even during the wait, that we stay focused. I remember when God first called me to be a Pastor in Jasper, FL, I had to go out and find an empty building. But in the midst of us being in the Scout Hut (our temporary place of worship) that God gave me the vision of having a church of my very own. In the vision, God gave me detail by detail of how to build the sanctuary and within a matter of months I had become an architect. I cannot boast of myself, because every detail that I drew out for the church, God gave it to me. He not only gave me the design of the church, but God also told me that in this transition would be debt free. Needless to say, I am excited and filled with exceeding joy. Then entered Satan. The building that we were currently occupying and had been renting from the City of Jasper was also being used for Boys and Girls Scout activities. Every so often I had to go before the board to extend our initial rental agreement. Now the first couple of extensions were a piece of cake, but after maybe the third or fourth extension it became an issue. They were giving us deadlines that we had to adhere to until finally, they told us to get out of the building altogether. I gathered all of the members of the church, even the youth, to attend the board meetings hoping that would help the board to have a little mercy on us and be considerate of our circumstance, but to my dismay they really wanted us gone. They told me of the many plans they had for the building and in their opinion, we were hindering those plans. Now the members of E.T.H.O.P heard all of this, they heard people stand up and call me a "lying preacher" and not only that, but outsiders also began to whisper about everything we were going through. As a Pastor, many people didn't know, but I honestly felt like the weight of the world was on my shoulders. I knew what God had shown me, and I knew that He had called me to preach the Gospel. Therefore, closing the doors of the church until we found a new building was not an option. So, I began to look for another building. How many of you know that God is a faithful and just God? His Divine Favor followed me, and I found a bigger building for a cheaper price. With the previous building we were only allowed to be in the building two days a week unless we receive special permission. But with this new building we would have access every day of the week as long as we wanted. I was saying to myself, "God is good". We went into that new building and cleaned it up from top to bottom. I had the church's decorating committee come in and work their magic, and they transitioned that building and made it look like a masterpiece. We were no longer renting from the City, but we became renters from the County. Life in the ministry was good again, our ministry really began to blossom. We were moving forward with the plans of our new church and, we were able to have church without hassle, so we thought. Then the architect we had working on our new church building pulled his license and all work on our church building had to cease until we could find a new one to come in. I was good with that, because we were still able to have church. We began to grace the front of the newspaper for the various activities our ministry was doing in the community, people were joining like never before and for once I felt like what the enemy had for our bad, God had turned it around for our good. Then entered Satan again. The County of Jasper decided that they wanted their building back so that they could make it into a museum for Hamilton County. I began to pray and say, "Not again God". The enemy wanted me to get angry, the enemy wanted me to fight back and neglect the Word of God that strictly instructed me to stand still and see the Salvation of the Lord. The same newspaper that we graced with good news was the same newspaper that wrote an article about our church being put out of the building we were in. I truly believe that the article was published as a form of embarrassment. This is when I began to notice the tactics of Satan, how he desires to keep us frustrated that we may lose focus on the plan that God really has for our lives.

Even in the midst of what we were facing, my heart went to Jehoshaphat in 2nd Chronicles 20th chapter. There was a group of people that consisted of the children of Moab, the children of Ammon, and the Bible tells us in 2 Chronicles 20:1 *"... and with them other beside the Ammonites, came against Jehoshaphat to battle."*. Now Jehoshaphat was facing a major problem, seeming like out of nowhere a multitude of people were ready to engage in battle with him. I read an article by Dr. Adrian Rogers entitled, *"How to Praise Your Way To Victory"* and this article so strategically talks about how Jehoshaphat at first did not see the solution for the problem that he was facing. What I have learned about battles, the enemy places people around you to help you engage in a spirit of fear. People were coming to tell Jehoshaphat what he was getting ready to face. The scripture states in 2 Chronicles 20:2 *"Then there came some that told Jehoshaphat, saying, There cometh a great multitude against thee from beyond the sea on this side Syria, and, behold, they be in Hazazontamar, which is Engedi"*. After hearing this news, the first emotion that we read about coming from Jehoshaphat was fear, but after the fear is the part that I love the most, the Bible lets us know that Jehoshaphat put a halt to everything, and he began to seek the Lord, but not only did he want to ensure a clear communication with the Lord, but he wanted that clear line for his people as well. He called a "nationwide" fast throughout all of Judah. This taught me a valuable lesson, some battles cannot be fought with an exchange of words, but to ensure a sound victory, praise needs to be involved. So,

Jehoshaphat according to the scripture stood in the congregation of Judah and Jerusalem and prayed a prayer like never before. Hold fast because now the story gets quite interesting. After the prayer was made, the Spirit of the Lord fell upon Jahaziel (the son of Zechariah, the son of Benaiah, the son of Jeiel, the son of Mattaniah, a Levite of the sons of Asaph) and a profound word was released from his mouth. 2 Chronicles 20:15 -17 states the words that were released from Jahaziel, "And he said, Hearken ye, all Judah, and ye inhabitants of Jerusalem, and thou king Jehoshaphat, Thus said the Lord unto you, Be not afraid nor dismayed by reason of this great multitude; for the battle is not yours, but God's. To morrow go ye down against them: behold, they come up by the cliff of Ziz; and ye shall find them at the end of the brook, before the wilderness of Jeruel. Ye shall not need to fight in this battle: set yourselves, stand ye still, and see the salvation of the Lord with you, O Judah and Jerusalem: fear not, nor be dismayed; to morrow go out against them: for the Lord will be with you" (www.oneplace.com).

Jehoshaphat full of joy, began to appoint singers that he knew would praise the Lord with everything that was in them. As a result of their obedience to the word of the Lord, when Jehoshaphat arrived at the battlefield, there was nothing left for them to do, but to rejoice in the goodness of the Lord for the scripture 2 Chronicles 20:

24 reads, "And when Judah came toward the watch tower in the wilderness, they looked unto the multitude, and, behold, they were dead bodies fallen to the earth, and none escaped". This is what victory resembles. They had to do absolutely nothing but sing praises unto the Lord and the Lord prevailed on their behalf. Now, I must ask a question that we hear so often, "Who wouldn't serve a God like this?"

After reading that scripture over and over, I even preached about it during watchnight service, I began to let the Word work for me. My wife, my awesome helpmeet in the ministry, started holding twelve o' clock prayer faithfully. She would get with some of the women of God, and they began to cry out to the Lord like never before. In the midst of their praying, God sent us another architecture that came on board which provided a license for us to continue working under for the rebuilding of our church. We were still going to board meeting after board meeting and finally they made a decision that we would have to leave that building. I was not upset, I rejoiced in the Lord because I know that it was God that called me to preach the Gospel, and this setback was not going to deter me from upholding what God entrusted me with. Once again, I began to look for another building. I had people coming up to me telling me that the people were wrong for putting us out, how we did not deserve to be handled in such a manner. I heard their words, but I stayed focused on God. I told the members of E.T.H.O.P. to refrain from speaking ill about the county officials, I told them to not even discuss the matter because I knew God was in control. I even took the newspaper article that was written about us and framed it because I knew that one day it was going to be used as a testimony. I found another building, this building had no affiliation with the county or the city, it was a single building that was being rented by one individual. This building came with two sides, one side that we were able to hold our regular services in and another section that the youth could use for various activities or if we were having a dinner we could dine in that area. I can honestly rejoice in the Lord especially when I look at our official church home which I

am proud to say estimated value is well over $100,000. –
Praise Break - If I would have quit after the first battle, my
eyes would have never rested upon what God really had
in store for the ministry. If I would have lost focus during
the second battle, I would not have been able to see the
spirit of excellency operate through the Saints of God at
E.T.H.O.P. I can honestly say, staying focused was truly
worth it because so much is dependent upon our
undivided attention.

Losing your focus during your wait can cause you
to act unseemly which goes against the will of God. I look
at Simon Peter who walked so closely with God. God
asked a very important question to the disciples in
Matthew 16:13, he asked, "...Whom do men say that I
the Son of man am?" Simple question that only required
a simple answer, but the answer could only be revealed
by the Father. Simon Peter boldly answered, "Thou art
the Christ, the Son of the living God". I can see the other
disciples probably wondering amongst themselves where
did Peter get an answer like that from, the answer to that

question so simple, the Father. From his response, Jesus was proud to declare unto Peter in Matthew 16:18-19:

> "And I say unto thee, That thou art Peter, and upon this rock I will build my church; and the gates of hell shall not prevail against it. And I will give unto thee the keys of the kingdom of heaven: and whatsoever thou shall bind on earth shall be bound in heaven; and whatsoever thou shalt loose on earth shall be loosed in heaven".

I read one man say that from this spoken word, Peter became an agent of divine revelation, but in order to fully operate in that capacity, Peter had to stay focused. He had to stay focused to every move that Jesus made, and not only every move, but every expression that was produced when Jesus came across opposition which would serve as a model to not only Peter, but the other disciples as well. Now let's fast forward to the garden of Gethsemane. The moment of opposition came, and it was proving time to see if they had really digested the wonderful things that had been either taught, they had seen or even just words that Jesus had spoken. Jesus foretold this day many times, telling the disciples (paraphrasing) that the hour was coming when the son of man would be betrayed. He told them that it was a must that He go away, and he even went on to say that when he left them, he wouldn't leave them comfortless, but that He would send them a comforter. But then came Judas (Iscariot), along with a band of men and officers from the chief priest and Pharisees, to fulfill what Jesus had been so vividly speaking about, and how did Peter react. Simon Peter reached in his belt, withdrew his sword, and took every ounce of strength he could muster up and cut the high priest's servant's right ear off. I could just imagine Jesus shaking his head and saying to himself, "Peter just learn how to wait, after while the world will see that I am the Son of God, after while they will see that I am the one that my Father sent to die for the sins of this wicked world – Peter stay focused and just wait!" Instead of acting irrationally Jesus just picked up the man's ear performed an awe-striking miracle and looked at Peter and according to Matthew 26:52-54 stated:

> "Then said Jesus unto him, Put up
> again thy sword into his place: for all they

that take the sword shall perish with the sword. Thinkest thou that I cannot now pray to my Father, and he shall presently give me more than twelve legions of angels? But how then shall the scriptures be fulfilled, that thus it must be"?

I know to some, this seem impossible, but you must STAY FOCUSED DURING THE WAIT. I can hear reoccurring accounts of every reason why not to wait, but the Word of the Lord gives us every reason why we should wait. Isaiah 40:31 states, *"But they that wait upon the Lord shall renew their strength; they shall mount up with wings as eagles; they shall run, and not be weary; and they shall walk, and not faint"*. God is faithful and just enough to forgive you when your patience gets thin and you act contrary to the Word of God, repentance may or may not be there, but even if you are forgiven just think about how one act of disobedience can make your journey so much longer. A breakthrough you could have received in thirty days, because of your reluctance to wait on God properly could take five years. I choose today to continue to wait on the Lord. During my wait I know that hard times will come, but I'm going to wait on the Lord. I know that some people may leave me that I want to stay, but I'm going to wait on the Lord. Because I declare and decree over my life today that my latter days will be greater than my former days.

CHAPTER 6

JESUS IS GREATER THAN ANYTHING

Should Believers ever turn away from their faith, or hold on to it? If so, why? My answer to the above question is yes, we must hold onto our faith no matter what. For the Bible declares: "Let us hold fast the confession of our hope without wavering, for He who promised is faithful; and let us consider how to stimulate one another to love and good deeds" (Hebrews 10:23–24). The book of Hebrews has a long list of reasons why we should cling to Jesus. Hebrews was written for Christians who had been in the church for a while. These folks knew about angels, the Old Testament heroes, the devil, and Moses. No other Book of the Bible so powerfully demonstrates Jesus' supremacy. Throughout Hebrews, the author compares Jesus to the heroes and icons of the Jewish faith. Each hero played a part, but His sacrifice, His covenant, and His current ministry are far greater than anything the others have to offer:

- Jesus is greater than the angels, because He is the divine King (Hebrews1:4, 6, 8).

- Jesus is greater than Moses, because while Moses was a servant of God, Jesus is the Son of God (Hebrew 3:3–4).
- Jesus is greater than Joshua, because Jesus brings a greater rest to the people of God (Hebrews 4:8–9).
- Jesus is a greater priest than Aaron, because He is sinless and immortal (Hebrews 7:26–28).

Not only is Jesus better than any other human religious figure, He also has a better ministry after ushering in a better covenant built on better promises with a better sacrifice, that is, Jesus Himself (Hebrews 7:22; 8:6; 9:12). The author of Hebrews encourages the Believers to join him in the following things:

- Holding fast to the confession—relying on Christ and not turning away from the faith (Hebrews 4:14, 10:23).
- Stimulating one another to love and good deeds— living in ways that demonstrate faith, obedience, thankfulness, reverence, and love (Hebrews 10:24).
- Apart from Romans, Hebrews is the most doctrine-heavy book of the New Testament. This book compellingly preaches and re-preaches Christ to those who know Him even today. No other book of the Bible so thoroughly explores Jesus' New Covenant and current priestly ministry like Hebrews.
- But that's not really what this book is famous for. Today, Christians immediately associate two things with the book of Hebrews: the mystery of who wrote it, and the "Hall of Faith."
- We don't know who wrote Hebrews. It could have been Barnabas, Priscilla, Apollos—it could have been almost anyone. Here's what we do know, though: Hebrews was likely written by someone who heard about Jesus after He ascended. The

author claims that salvation was first spoken through Jesus, then through those who heard Jesus. "Those who heard" then performed signs, wonders, and miracles (Hebrews 2:3–4).

- The author of Hebrews puts himself in a third category of people who heard about Jesus second-hand. This would exclude Paul, who specifically says he did not receive the gospel from men, but from Jesus Himself (Galatians 1:12). Besides, the feel of Hebrews is quite different from that of the Pauline epistles.

- Hebrews is also well known for its eleventh chapter, which has been nicknamed the "Hall of Faith." This chapter is a long list of Old Testament characters who, through faith, accomplished great things and bore up under great tribulation. This chapter cites Abraham, Moses, many characters from the book of Judges, and others as examples of what God can accomplish through our faith.

- Both points of interest (the mystery of authorship and the compelling presentation of content) may stem from Hebrew's original nature. Many scholars believe Hebrews was first written as a sermon (or series of sermons) to a congregation. When the sermon was distributed to other churches, an epistle-sounding conclusion may have been added to the end. This could explain why there is no formal introduction to this letter like the ones we see in every other NT epistle.

- We don't know who wrote the book of Hebrews.

- Tradition holds that the book of Hebrews was written to Christian (surprise, surprise!) Hebrews. The author never explicitly says the audience is Jewish, but does assume that the audience is intimately familiar with the Old Testament, especially the Pentateuch.

- Even so, this epistle is, I believe, one of God's greatest gifts to His church: an expository look at the person, life, covenant, sacrifice, and ministry of the Lord Jesus Christ, who is indeed greater than all others (overviewbible.com).

I remember back on December 28th, 2008, I preached a sermon by the name of, "Jesus is Greater Than Anything" coming from the scripture John 10:10 which reads, "The thief cometh not, but for to steal, and to kill, and to destroy: I am come that they might have life, and that they might have it more abundantly." In this sermon I began to say that Jesus is greater than sin. He is so wide, that you can't go around Him, so low that you can't go under Him, so high that you can't go above Him. Jesus is greater than depression, our shortcoming, Jesus is greater than…. You are going to be tried in this world, but God will prepare you and make you ready. We must change our focus and reverence God more than the devil, why, because Jesus is greater than…. Stop giving up so easy. The enemy comes to steal, kill and destroy, but Jesus came that we may have life and have it more abundantly. We are clean, but that is not good enough. We are cleaned on the outside, but we have hidden stuff that is way deep on the inside. We need to work on us and tell God, it's me and nobody else that is standing in the need of prayer. Confess your sins before God and allow Him to clean you up from the inside out. We have to give up ourselves. We must get rid of ourselves and let the blood of Jesus wash away our sins. It's so clear to me that God used me to speak His words eight years ago and I still hold fast to that title today: "Jesus is Greater Than Anything". I am not just focusing on just professing that name (Jesus), but the lifestyle that is accompanied by that name. Jesus is greater than anything!!

The Word of God displays so many situations that further indicates the power of just a single touch from Jesus which supersedes anything that may come against us. One passage of scripture that I love to read about is the woman that had an issue of blood for twelve long years. I have encountered a couple of women in my life that have suffered from this same ailment and the only thing that worked for them was some type of surgical procedure. Once the procedure was completed the issue ceased. With careful examination of this particular scripture, it is learned that no surgical procedure was skillful enough to bring an end to her ongoing problem. The Bible lets us know in Mark 5:25-26, "And a certain woman, which had an issue of blood twelve years, And had suffered many things of many physicians, and had spent all that she had, and was nothing bettered, but rather grew worse." Jesus is greater than anything. Now if we were to examine her issue, this very act should not have even happened. According to the Old Testament, a woman that had an issue of blood was deemed as unclean and was separated from others. Leviticus 15:19 reads, "And if a woman have an issue, and her issue in her flesh be blood, she shall be put apart seven days, and whosoever touchest her shall be unclean until the even", after reading that scripture the mere fact that this woman was found in a crowd, pressing and pushing trying to make it to Jesus lets me know that she tapped in to the power that Jesus possessed. She didn't make a scene, she didn't even attempt to yell his name, all she did was touch the helm of His garment. The Bible tells us in Mark 5:28, "For she said, If I may touch but his clothes,

I shall be whole". If this scripture would have continued, I can imagine in my spirit her stating, "because I know that Jesus, yes Jesus, is greater than anything". By her obeying what she believed in healing came immediately.

In the decisions that we make, God wants to see if we whole heartedly believe that He is greater than anything. When I really began working, I had some great offers from some well-paying jobs. Just think, I was nineteen years old, had a wife, and a son, so I needed a job that paid well so I could properly take care of my family. I had Roadway offering almost fifteen dollars an hour, and back in the late 80's that was real good money, I had a place called Occidental that came with a pretty good salary, then I had a janitorial position at the school which salary wasn't the best, but it was a job. I contemplated those jobs until my head started hurting, but I wouldn't make a decision until I talked to my father-in-law who was also my Pastor, my spiritual leader. He began to tell me that those other jobs were good, but the schedules were unpredictable which would make me miss a lot of church, but at least at the school (money may not be what I wanted), I could be in church, and children needed to be in school which was a secured position. Once he released those words my mind was made up completely, I took the job at the school. I was off on the weekends, but if I remember correctly my schedule was from two in the evening to ten at night. Just sticking to that schedule, I would be off on Sunday's but those during the week church services I would miss, or at least so the devil thought. I was so purpose driven and determined to prove how great God was to me, I would not take a lunch break at my normal time, but I would take it around 6:30pm and use that time to go to church and when church was over, I went back to work. I went in (during the week services) my Dickie slacks and shirt and my work boots ready to praise God. Then one day, the Spirit took completely over me, and I began to say that God was going to loose me from that job so that I could be in church the way I desired to be. I tell you the honest truth, within a week I received a call from my supervisor asking me what I wanted my new shift time to be. At first,

I thought that I was hearing incorrectly so I asked her to repeat herself to me again. When I heard her reiterate her original words I said in my spirit, Jesus you are greater than anything. I initially told her I wanted five in the morning to one o' clock in the afternoon. Since the school they had chosen to put me in buses didn't come until 1:45pm she said that if I could adjust my time to 1:45pm we had a deal. I was so overjoyed. I never doubt God's Word, but it is a blessing when He can work a miracle in your favor. Some may read my story and say that could have happened to anybody, but I beg to differ, when you are faithful to God, He in turn becomes faithful to you. When you put Him first, and delight yourself in Him regardless of your circumstance, He will give you the desires of your heart.

As I looked at the woman that had the issue of blood circumstance, I can so vividly see that assurance brings forth action. She was sure of the power that was invested in Jesus, she was sure that she would be healed, and she was sure that there was a need. I can fathom every excuse she could have mustered up to turn around and walk away. I can imagine her saying, "It's too many people around Jesus, I'll just wait until He comes around again" or "Oh God, what if people see me and notice my issue, what will they say about me", (sounds exactly like some of the ineffective excuses we come up with when our healing is at hand). And she would have been absolutely correct if she made mention of the crowd because the Bible says that there was a multitude (Mark 5:31). This is why I make mention of assurance, she was assured that Jesus is greater than anything, so she called her mind to come into subjection to the Word of God and action was produced: she touched his garment. Then the words that she had been longing to hear for twelve years escaped the mouth of Jesus, Mark 5:34, "...Daughter, thy faith hath made thee whole; go in peace, and be whole of thy plague". In a matter of minutes, she went from being an outcast to being a testimony. She went from being an ordinary woman with an issue, to woman that the world would forever read about. The same way that God moved in her life, He is waiting to move in our life, but what move are we willing to make. Are we fully convinced that Jesus is greater than anything? Are we fully convinced that we can be the head and not the tail? Are we fully convinced that we can be the lender and not the borrower? If you can answer yes to any one of those questions, you need to allow your assurance to bring forth action and move towards God.

I say this to you: Jesus is all that we need, and He is so much that we cannot afford to put Him in a box. How can you describe someone who is everything wrapped up in one name – Jesus! God wants us to stand in order to get some standards. We cannot stay in the same state; we must go higher. It's a bad thing to see the Promised Land that is flowing with milk and honey, but not touch it. I AM says that you will be able to bring life to dead situations. Therefore, don't let any form of hindrance hinder you from getting what God has for you. I AM is able to take care of anything that you may encounter. Whatever you need, I AM has it. If I can't get it or if it doesn't exist, I AM will create it. Stand on the Word of God. Don't put anything, absolutely anything before

Jesus. If ye be in Christ you, are a new creature

therefore, begin to speak life to yourself and confess I

believe in the power of I AM.

For your leisure, study the following scriptures

because in order to declare that Jesus is greater than

anything, you must first know who Jesus is.

- John 8:25 – Then said they unto him, Who art thou? And Jesus saidth unto them, Even the same that I said unto you from the beginning.

- John 6:35 – And Jesus said unto them, I am the Bread of Life: he that cometh to Me shall never hunger; and he that believeth on Me shall never thirst.

- John 8:12 – Then spake Jesus again unto them, saying, I am the Light of the world: he that followeth Me shall not walk in darkness, but shall have the light of life.

- John 10:7 and 9 – Then said Jesus unto them again, Verily, verily, I say unto you, I am the door of the sheep. I am the door: by me if any man enter in, he shall be saved, and shall go in and out, and find pasture.

- John 11:25 – Jesus said unto her, I am the Resurrection, and the Life: no man cometh unto the Father, but by Me.

- John 15:1 – I am the true vine, and my Father

  is the husbandman.

We must love Jesus not only more than our families but more than our own lives. The moment we become Christ's followers, our own lives and wills become forfeit; we die with Christ to sin (that is, to the right to make selfish choices; Romans 6:3-4) and choose a path that could lead any day to our execution for Christ's name (Matthew 16:24). The promise of eternal life should be sufficient motivation for any who genuinely believe in Jesus - it doesn't take a rocket scientist to recognize that the greatest mortal longevity pales in comparison with eternity-but we sometimes prove less committed than we suppose (Matthew 26:41). That even the first disciples were not initially prepared for such a demand (Matthew 26:56) does not mitigate the level of commitment our Lord seeks from us: if we want to be followers of Jesus, we must be ready to die. In other words, I value my life in this world more than I value Jesus and the life of the next world; I am not worthy to be His disciple. We need not worry about who we are, what we can do or what we can't do. On the contrary, we should be more concerned about who God is.

CHAPTER 7

WE MUST HAVE A WILLING SPIRIT

"I will most gladly spend and be completely spent for your souls," wrote the apostle Paul (2 Corinthians 12:15). What do these words tell you about the outlook and attitude that God's servants should try to cultivate? According to several bible scholars, when Paul wrote those words to the Christians in Corinth, he was saying: "I am willing to spend my strength, and time, and life, and all that I have for your welfare, as a father cheerfully does for his children." Paul was prepared to "be completely exhausted and worn out," if that's what it would take to fulfill his ministry. Moreover, Paul did all of this 'with gladness'. He was willing to do so. What about you? Are you willing to spend your time, energy, talents, and resources serving Jehovah God and the interests of others, even if doing so means being "exhausted and worn out" at times? And would you do it all "with gladness"?

Most individuals refuse to serve God. Their spirit is one of selfish independence and rebellion. Satan enticed

Adam and Eve into this same type of thinking. He wrongly said that they would "be like God, knowing good and bad"—able to decide for themselves what is right and what is wrong (Genesis 3:1-5). Those who have the same spirit today think that they should have complete freedom to do exactly what they desire without any obligation to God or interference from Him (Psalm 81:11, 12). They want to use all that they possess in the pursuit of their own personal interests (Proverbs 18:1). You probably do not share this extreme view. Likely you genuinely appreciate the gift of life you now enjoy and the even more wonderful prospect of living forever (Psalm 37:10, 11; Revelation 21:1-4). You may be deeply grateful to God our Father for His goodness to you. But all of us need to be alert to the danger that Satan can distort our thinking in such a way that our service may actually become unacceptable to God (2 Corinthians 11:3). How might this happen? God wants willing, wholehearted service. He never forces us to do His will. It is Satan who will stop at nothing to pressure or entice people into doing wrong. In connection with serving God, the Bible does speak of obligation, commandments, requirements, and so forth (Ecclesiastes 12:13; Luke 1:6). Yet, our primary motive for serving God should be because we love Him (Exodus 35:21; Deuteronomy 11:1). Regardless of how much Paul spent himself in God's service, he knew that this would mean nothing at all 'if he did not have love' (1 Corinthians 13:1-3). When Bible writers refer to Christians as slaves of God, they are not referring to abject servitude based on coercion (Romans 12:11; Colossians 3:24). What is meant is willing subjection based on deep, heartfelt love for God and His Son, Jesus (Matthew 22:37; 2 Corinthians 5:14; 1 John 4:10, 11).

The Holy Spirit told me to tell you, that you must have a willing spirit. Whatever you give out, is what will come back to you. Do you know that we are nasty? Let me explain. The Bible declares that we were born in sin and shaped in iniquity thus making us nasty. Therefore, when God cleans you up, don't cast your pearls to the swine. 2 Corinthians 9:6-7 says,

Now [remember] this: he who sows sparingly will also reap sparingly, and he who sows generously [that blessings may come to others] will also reap generously [and be blessed]. Let each one give [thoughtfully and with purpose] just as he has decided in his heart, not grudgingly or under compulsion, for God loves a cheerful giver [and delights in the one whose heart is in his gift].

You must have a willing spirit. In other words, your spirit must become agreeable to the Word of God. Jesus became poor, so that we through His poverty might become rich. You have to have readiness of mind in order to do what God asks you to do. Everybody is not going to have the same mindset. But thank God for the mind that you do have. We look for perfection in the church based on our standards and our desires. And when the church does not meet your criteria, you search for a place that does. But what we must realize is this; it's not about us, it's about God. Ask God for a willing spirit, and He will give it to you.

2 Corinthians 8:8-12 says this:

I am not saying this as a command [to dictate to you], but to prove, by [pointing out] the enthusiasm of others, the sincerity of your love as well. For you are recognizing [more clearly] the grace of our Lord Jesus Christ [His astonishing kindness, His generosity, His gracious favor], that though He was rich, yet for your sake He became poor, so that by His poverty you might become rich (abundantly blessed). I give you my opinion in this matter: this is to your advantage, who were the first to begin a year ago not only to take action [to help the believers in Jerusalem], but also [the first] to desire *to do it*. So now finish this, so that your eagerness in desiring it may be equaled by your completion of it, according to your ability. For if the eagerness [to give] is there, it is acceptable according to what one has, not according to what he does not have.

Our service to God must also reflect a deep love for people. "We must become gentle in His midst, as when a nursing mother cherishes her own children," wrote Paul to the congregation in Thessalonica (1 Thessalonians 2:7). By law, mothers have a legal obligation to take care of their children. But surely most mothers do not do this just because it's the law, do they? No. They do it because they love and cherish their children; a mother gladly makes sacrifices for her children. Because Paul had a similar "tender affection" for those he ministered to, he was pleased to use his very

120

life in helping them (1 Thessalonians 2:8). Love motivates us to follow Paul's example (Matthew 22:39). Of course, we must not let love of self-outweigh the love of God and people. Otherwise, there is a real danger that we may render only half-hearted, reluctant service. We could even begin to develop some resentment, feeling upset that we cannot live our lives according to our own desires. This happened to some Israelites who lost their love for God but still rendered some service to Him out of a sense of duty. What was the result? Serving God became "a weariness" to them (Malachi 1:13).

Any offerings made to God should always be without defect – the best we have to offer (Leviticus 22:17-20; Exodus 23:19). Instead of giving God the best of their animals, however, people in Malachi's day began to offer those they really did not want themselves. What was God's reaction? He told the priests: "When you present a blind animal for sacrificing (you say): 'It is nothing bad.' And when you present a lame animal or a sick one: 'It is nothing bad.' Bring it near, please, to your governor. Will he find pleasure in you, or will he receive you kindly? . . . And you have brought something torn away, and the lame one, and the sick one; yes, you have brought it as a gift. "Can I take pleasure in it at your hand" (Malachi 1:8, 13)? How might this happen to any of us? Our sacrifices might become "a weariness" to us if we lack a truly willing heart and spirit (Exodus 35:5, 21, 22, Leviticus 1:3, Psalm 54:6, Hebrews 13:15, 16). For example, does God get the leftovers of our time? Can anyone seriously think that it would have been acceptable to God if a well-meaning family member or a zealous Levite somehow forced an unwilling Israelite to select his best animal for sacrifice when he really did not want to offer it (Isaiah 29:13, Matthew 15:7, 8)? God rejected such sacrifices and eventually the people who offered them (Hosea 4:6; Matthew 21:43). To offer God service that He will accept, we must follow the example of Jesus Christ. "I seek, not my own will," he said, "but the will of Him that sent me" (John 5:30). Jesus found great happiness in willingly serving God. Jesus fulfilled David's prophetic words: "To do Your will, O my God, I have delighted"(Psalm 40:8). Although Jesus delighted to do God's will, does not mean that it was always easy. Consider what happened just before His arrest, trial, and execution. While in the Garden of Gethsemane, Jesus was deeply grieved and agonized over the cup of suffering He was about to drink of. So intense was the emotional pressure that, as He prayed, "His sweat became as drops of blood falling to the ground" (Matthew 26:38; Luke 22:44). Why did Jesus experience such agony? Certainly not because of reluctance to do God's will. He was prepared to die, even reacting strongly to Peter's words: "Be kind to yourself, Lord; you will not have this destiny at all" (Matthew 16:21-23). We may never fully understand Jesus' agony in the Garden of Gethsemane, but what we do know is this. It was that agony of God and man in one Person, coming face to face with sin.

Jesus was aware that His Father would be greatly pained to see His Beloved Son treated in a barbaric fashion. Jesus also understood that he was approaching a pivotal time in the outworking of God's purpose. Faithfully adhering to God's laws would demonstrate beyond a shadow of doubt that Adam could have made the same choice. Jesus' faithfulness exposed as entirely false Satan's assertion that humans under test could not faithfully and willingly serve God. By means of Jesus, God ultimately crushed Satan and removed the effects of his rebellion (Genesis 3:15). What an enormous responsibility that rested on Jesus' shoulders! His Father's Name, universal peace, and the Salvation of mankind all depended on Jesus' faithfulness. Knowing this, He prayed: "My Father, if it is possible, let this cup pass away from me. Yet, not as I will, but as you will" (Matthew 26:39). Even under the severest stress, Jesus never faltered in His willingness to submit to His Father's will. Inasmuch as Jesus suffered intense emotional stress as He served God, we can expect Satan to exert pressure on us as God's servants (John 15:20; 1 Peter 5:8). Moreover, we are imperfect. So even if we willingly serve God, it will not be easy for us to do so. Jesus saw how His disciples struggled to do all that He asked them to do. That is why He said: "The spirit, of course, is willing, but the flesh is weak" (Matthew 26:41). "There was nothing inherently weak in His perfect human flesh. However, He had in mind the weakness of His disciples' flesh, the imperfection that they had inherited from imperfect Adam" (MacArthur: 32). Jesus knew that because of inherited imperfection and resulting human limitations, they would have a struggle to do all they wanted to in God's service. So, then, we may feel like the apostle Paul, who was deeply distressed when imperfection inhibited his ability to serve God fully. "Ability to wish is present with me," Paul wrote, "but ability to work out what is fine is not present" (Romans 7:18). We too find that we cannot carry out completely all the good things we wish to do (Romans 7:19). This is not because of any reluctance on our part. It is simply because the weakness of the flesh hinders even our best efforts. But do not despair. If we have heartfelt readiness to do all we can, God will surely accept our service (2 Corinthians 8:12). May we 'do our utmost' to imitate Christ's spirit of complete submission to God's will (2 Timothy 2:15; Philippians 2:5-7; 1 Peter 4:1, 2). God will reward and support such a willing spirit. He will give us "the power beyond what is normal" to compensate for our weaknesses (2 Corinthians 4:7-10). With God's help we, like Paul, will most gladly spend our time and energy in His precious service.

> "Create in me a pure heart, O God, and renew a steadfast spirit within me. Do not cast me from your presence or take your Holy Spirit from me. Restore to me the joy of your salvation and grant me a willing spirit, to sustain me. Then I will teach transgressors your ways, so that sinners will turn back to you" (Psalm 51-10-13).

After receiving the Lord Jesus into our heart as our Lord and Savior at the time of our regeneration, we Believers became different. We are no longer merely men, we are God-men and women, Christ-men and women, and Spirit-men and women. We now have the Triune God living within us. And in everything we do, we learn to turn to Him for direction and guidance. We no longer live a worldly-carefree life because we are spirit filled men and women. In Psalm 51 we see that David prayed to the Lord concerning three kinds of spirit(s): a steadfast spirit, a willing spirit, and a broken spirit. We need the Lord to renew a steadfast spirit within us (Psalm

51:10), we need Him to sustain us with a willing spirit (Psalm 51:12), and we need to have a broken and repentant spirit (Psalm 51:17) so that God may be pleased with us. In Psalm 51:10 David prays, Create in me a clean heart, O God, and renew a steadfast spirit within me. In other versions we read, a right spirit – but the best way to translate this word is steadfast, upright, or firm. Because David did not have a steadfast and firm spirit, he fell and committed the sin of adultery. We need to have an upright spirit, a steadfast spirit, a spirit that is immovable, unshakable, standing constantly firm and steady.

Just like David, we need to repent of our sins and ask the Lord to renew a right spirit within us. In order for us to never be seduced or misled in our Christian life and walk, we always need to have an upright spirit, a spirit which is steadfast, firm, constant, immovable, and unshakable. (See 1 Corinthians 15:58) This means that we will not be fluctuating up and down but regardless of the situations or circumstances, we will be steadfast in spirit and unmovable always abounding in Him. Lord

Jesus, create in us a clean heart and cleanse our hearts, of any impurities and evil thoughts or desires; renew a steadfast spirit within us. Restore to me the gladness of Your Salvation and sustain me with a willing spirit" (Psalm 51:12). Although we do things for the Lord; working in the church and doing outreach ministry we may not always have a willing spirit. But when we have the joy of the Lord and Salvation, we will spontaneously have a willing spirit to do whatever He wants us to do.

As Believers, we should always have a willing spirit for the things of the Lord and for the things of the church. When we sin or stray away from the Lord, and lose our joy, we should repent and ask the Lord to restore to us the joy of His Salvation, so that we may be strengthened. When we have joy in the Spirit (Romans 14:17), we will have a willing spirit to fellowship with the Lord, worship Him, pray, meet with the saints, prophesy, serve in the church life, etc. Whatever pleases the Lord, we will be happy to do! "The sacrifices of God are a broken spirit; a broken and a contrite heart, O God, You will not despise" (Psalm 51:17). God who created the

Heaven and earth delights to look and be with a man with a broken and contrite spirit (Isaiah 66:2). In God's eyes, a broken spirit is more precious than sacrifices. Having a broken spirit doesn't mean that your spirit is broken in pieces – it means that your spirit is not whole, not complete, but is a repenting spirit. David had a big failure, and he had a broken and repentant spirit. We may not have such big failures and sins, but in the Lord's light we see our sins, weaknesses, defects, and failures. We should not consider ourselves as perfect and complete, but rather humble ourselves and have a repenting spirit, confessing to the Lord our weaknesses and failures. When we repent, our spirit is contrite, broken, and feeling sorrowful. The Lord needs to recover in us a repentant spirit. We may not sin in a great way, but quite often we are wrong in our words, our attitude, our desires, our feelings, our thoughts, our talking to others, our doing things, etc. Even unconsciously we are wrong. We need not ever consider ourselves as being complete, whole, or perfect. No one is perfect; we are still sinful, and we need to always repent and confess our sins and short comings before the Lord. We are lacking; we are not perfect; we are not complete; we are contrite and ready to repent. O Lord, we need you so much!

I have a saying that I use in our ministry, and I say, "This is not Burger King, you cannot have it your way". When it comes to God and His will, our flesh must die and once our flesh dies our spirit must become willing. I know that sounds so crazy and far-fetched because when we began to profess God, we are so quick to say, "God whatever you have me to do, I'm willing", and the enemy laughs because he knows that is so far from the truth. But a willing spirit is a factor that can separate us from greatness. When God first placed in my spirit that we must have a willing spirit my mind quickly went to when Jesus was praying in the Garden of Gethsemane. Jesus knew that the time was approaching for him to be crucified, and that this suffering would affect him physically, emotionally, and spiritually and this was something that caused Jesus to become sorrowful. Knowing and understanding the power of prayer, Jesus took Peter and the two sons of Zebedee and he entered into prayer. Initially Jesus was expecting those that were with Him to go into prayer with Him, the Bible tells us in Matthew 26:38, "Then saith he unto them, My soul is exceeding sorrowful, even unto death: tarry ye here, and watch with me". It is so clear to me why those that were with Jesus didn't see the need to continue in prayer, they couldn't foresee the suffering of Jesus Christ. It became so intense that the Bible further tells us in Matthew 26:39: "And he went a little further, and fell on his face, and prayed, saying, O my Father, if it be possible, let this cup pass from me: nevertheless, not as I will, but as thou wilt". This shows me that Jesus stopped relying on his flesh and submitted to the will of His Father. I fully understand that our flesh is so limited, and it does not want to go through anything. Our flesh does not want to humble, our flesh doesn't want to suffer, to put it plainly, our flesh doesn't want to do anything that is lined up with the Word of God. Jesus realized that even though He had supreme power, He was not going to rely on His flesh for the transition that God was taking Him through. He needed the Spirit. Jesus began to say in the latter part of Matthew 26:41, "the spirit is indeed willing, but the flesh is weak."

When we rely on the Spirit, there are promises that comes with a willing spirit. In order to receive those promises of God, we need to drop our ways for Jesus' ways. The enemy laughs at our weakness and the decisions that we make through our flesh. But when our spirit becomes willing, we are able to destroy everything around us with the power that God grants us from Heaven. When we develop a willing spirit, we can rely on Jesus to be five things in our lives:

- A Counselor – a person who advises; a person in charge; someone who can speak or stand up for you.

- Helper – to give or do something that is needed or useful; makes things easier for. We all have needs and we need Jesus to do something for us. Where would we be if Jesus didn't supply all of our needs (not our wants)? Jesus came to help us and to set us free. He came to loose the shackles that has us bound He will help you out.

- Intercessor – A person who is interceding; who intercedes; travailing. To act or to plead on the behalf of another. To act in agreement – Why do you come to church? Just to be mediocre? You should want to be great in God. If you don't ever become great in God, how will you know how great God is?

- Strengthener – to make one strong
- Standby – to be near or ready if needed. To help support; to be a sign of representation.

Growing up I had the worst temper that a young man could possess. I didn't engage in arguments, while the other person would be arguing, I would be in position to fight. That's why I believe many people developed the theory that I wouldn't live long, because they were judging me according to my temper. They believed two things, either I would kill someone, or someone would kill me. When I turned my life over to God, He still had work to do with my temper, but I am thankful that I had good leaders teaching me the proper way to handle things. When I first began working at the school, I had an assignment of working every other Saturday with the prisoners. Even if my supervisor didn't keep up with my Saturday schedule, I made sure I did. One Saturday, I had planned to spend some family time with my wife and son since I was off, but early that morning my supervisor called and asked why I hadn't showed up to work yet. In the beginning of the conversation, I was very polite, trying to explain that I had worked the last Saturday, so this was my Saturday to be off. It seemed the more that I tried to express myself in a polite way, the harsher my supervisor became, and I could feel my temper rising. Before I could get out of myself, my mother-in-law Church Mother Daniels, was in the background telling me to humble myself. I looked at her so crazy and, in my mind, I'm asking, "humble to what, I'm the one right", and she said it again, "humble yourself son". I told the supervisor that I would see him in a few and I hung up the phone. She began to let me know the importance of my flesh dying, I knew and most importantly God knew the temper that I was battling with so sometimes in order for deliverance to have its perfect work, we have to be tried in that area. Before long, my spirit became willing, I humbled myself to what my church mother told me, and I walked on that job ready to work. After being there for almost an hour, the supervisor came up to me and apologized, recognizing that I really was supposed to have that Saturday off. I told him it was okay, and I went ahead and finished that day out. That situation taught me a valuable lesson. Sometimes, even when we become saved, our flesh fights against doing what is right. We will reach back and grab old ways and become fighters of battles that don't even belong to us. But when our spirit becomes willing, we are willing to fight against our flesh and act according to how the Word says that we should act. Even if we are right, our spirit should still be willing to humble. Even when we feel like we don't deserve it, our spirit should still be willing to go through. That is an attribute that we so clearly seen in Jesus, His willing spirit.

After Jesus prayed to His Father, Matthew 26:42 shows when the flesh gave up and the Spirit stepped in, "He went away again the second time, and prayed, saying, O my Father, if this cup may not pass away from me, except I drink it, thy will be done." He no longer worried about the disciples staying awake and praying with Him, there was a mandate upon Jesus' life, He couldn't change it because the Word of God had to be fulfilled. That's exactly how it is with us. There are some things that we just have to go through, and we can't do it through our flesh, but it takes a willing spirit. We must become secure in our position with Jesus, He has our back, and we really don't have to be troubled by anything. We cannot change anything, some things we are going to have to go through, but God is so good because He is able to bring us through. If God did not think we could handle it, He would not put us through it. If God did not think that Jesus could handle the crucifixion, He would not have put Him through it. Just think of all of the other Biblical leaders in the Bible that God could have used, but He chose His Son because for number one, no sin could be found in Jesus and number two, He knew that His son had a willing spirit. Now all the places I used Jesus' name in for the sentences below use your name. God would not put certain things on

_____ if He knew that _____could

not take it. What makes our going through so much

easier is when our spirit becoming willing to the will of

God.

CHAPTER 8

DEALING WITH FRUSTRATION

We live in a world full of challenges, dangers and stress. Can faith really overcome our frustrations? Millions of people around the world suffer from anxiety disorders. TIME Magazine asked the question, how many of us are "worrying ourselves sick"? That article observed, "There is certainly a lot of anxiety going around. Anxiety disorder - which is what health experts call any anxiety that persists to the point that it interferes with one's life - is the most common mental illness in the U.S. Many people experience even more serious mental health challenges, including panic attacks or panic disorder. The National Institute of Mental Health reported that approximately 2.4 million American adults ages 18 to 54, or about 1.7 percent of people in this age group in a given year, have panic disorder. Millions of us experience anxieties that interfere with normal living. Just the stress of everyday life can kill us. We commute in congested traffic. We interact with angry, argumentative people. We face financial, social and personal problems.

The Bible gives us strategies for overcoming worries, frustrations, and anxieties. But our materialistic world distracts us from spiritual priorities. Jesus chastised His listeners who worried about food and clothing. He said, "Now if God so clothes the grass of the field, which today is, and tomorrow is thrown into the oven, will He not much more clothe you, O you of little faith?" (Matthew 6:30). Yet many of us allow ourselves to worry. We become fearful and anxious. What do Americans fear most?

> A 2001 Gallup Poll surveyed U.S. adults about their fears. The number one fear was snakes, affecting 51 percent; the second-most prominent fear was public speaking, affecting 40 percent. These were followed by: heights: 36 percent; enclosure in a small space: 34 percent; spiders and insects: 27 percent; needles and shots: 21 percent; mice: 20 percent; flying: 18 percent; thunder and lightning: 11 percent; dogs: 11 percent; crowds: 11 percent; going to the doctor: 9 percent; the dark: 5 percent (www.gotquestions.org).

God knows our fears. Jesus said that your Father knows you intimately. Jesus gives us this encouraging perspective and instruction: "Are not five sparrows sold for two copper coins? And not one of them is forgotten before God. But the very hairs of your head are all numbered. Do not fear; therefore, you are of more value than many sparrows" (Luke 12:6–7). Or, as the NIV states it: "Don't be afraid; you are worth more than many sparrows" (Luke 12:7). As you read and study God's word—the Bible – you will learn of His awesome love and His amazing promises to you. You will find documentation of God's intervention in people's lives. He promises that He will intervene in your life! Just read Jesus' words in chapters 5–7 of Matthew's gospel, often called "The Sermon on the Mount". Today, there are so many distractions that keep us from spiritual priorities. We live in a materialistically minded world. Many folks seek wealth as their first goal in life, whether possessions of real estate, cars, boats, jewelry, cash, or designer clothing. Others seek power of position in government, business, or education. And even yet, others seek pleasure through illicit sex, overindulgence in media and other forms of entertainment, alcohol, or illegal drugs. Many have even become addicted to video games. Human nature causes us to turn to activities that deepen our fears and our frustrations. How can we replace those fears and frustrations with peace, faith and love?

If we have reverence for God, we can keep our daily problems in perspective. Many in mainstream churches call the fear of God "primitive". But the biblical fear of God is not "being afraid" of Him – it is a deep reverence and respect for our Creator. It is an awe of God's majesty and greatness. It is a response to the reality of God. When you choose to fear God, you will not fear human beings. We must understand that the *fear* of God and the *love* of God are not mutually exclusive. Many professing Christians think that you have one or the other. That is not what your Bible says. Both qualities are required in our relationship with God.

"And now, Israel, what does the Lord your God require of you but to   fear the Lord your God, to walk in all his ways and to love Him, to serve the
Lord your God with all your heart and with all your soul, and to keep the   commandments of the Lord

141

and His statutes which command you today for your good" (Deuteronomy 10:12–13)?

A godly fear helps us overcome phobias and worries. "In the fear of the Lord there is strong confidence, and His children will have a place of refuge" (Proverbs 14:26). True faith and confidence-strong confidence-come from God. The New Testament also praises the value of a godly fear. Notice: "By faith Noah, being divinely warned of things not yet seen, moved with godly fear, prepared an ark for the saving of his household, by which he condemned the world and became heir of the righteousness which is according to faith" (Hebrews 11:7). Yes, God requires that we both love Him *and* fear Him. Both qualities go hand in hand! I challenge you to read through the books of Psalms and Proverbs. The blessings and benefits of a godly fear will amaze you! How else can we overcome our worries and anxieties? Jesus' beloved apostle, John, wrote: "There is no fear in love; but perfect love casts out fear, because fear involves torment" (1 John 4:18). Love is the antidote to fear. How can we have that love? We must realize the profound truth John mentions: God is love. "And we have known and believed the love that God has for us. God is love, and he who abides in love abides in God, and God in him" (1 John 4:16).

Yes, God loves us, and He will give us the gift of His spiritual love! He gives us this amazing promise: "And hope putteth not to shame; because the love of God hath been shed abroad in our hearts through the Holy Spirit which was given unto us" (Romans 5:5). Our selfish-human nature can be transformed into a loving, godly nature. We receive this precious gift of godly love by the Holy Spirit that was given to us. On the day of Pentecost, the Apostle Peter explained to thousands how to receive this wonderful gift: "Then Peter said to them, 'Repent, and let every one of you be baptized in the name of Jesus Christ for the remission of sins; and you shall receive the gift of the Holy Spirit. For the promise is to you and to your children, and to all who are afar off, as many as the Lord our God will call" (Acts 2:38–39).

Sometimes, Christians are not close to God, and they become frustrated. "The word "frustrate" means "to prevent from attaining a purpose; to thwart". The word comes from the French *frustra* which means "in vain" (www. Biblescripture.net). The fruits of frustration can include mental anxiety, worry, turmoil, apprehension, nervousness, and restlessness. How can we overcome our frustrations? Many of us live lives of worry and anxiety. We all experience frustration in our modern society. We sit in traffic jams when we are late for an appointment. We feel burdened with long hours on the job. We may feel rejected when asking someone for a date. We may feel insecure, or unloved. We may have conflicts with friends or family. We may have health problems. We may lack patience. Things just go badly for us at our workplace, or school. Why do we experience so many frustrations? Perhaps our focus is on the material rather than the spiritual. What goals are you setting? When you set the wrong goal, you can be thwarted and frustrated. The simple solution is to *set the right goal*. If you have not already internalized these words of Jesus, you should: "Seek first the kingdom of God and His righteousness, and all these things shall be added to you" (Matthew 6:33). We become frustrated when we have the wrong goal, or no goal at all. God has made us for an awesome purpose. When we commit to His goal, and seek God's Kingdom and His righteousness, we minimize life's frustrations! We also become frustrated when we insist that our own will be done, without consideration for others. The selfish attitude is, "I want it my way". Our Savior gave us the right example. Even when He faced crucifixion, He prayed, "Father, if it is Your will, take this cup away from Me; nevertheless, not My will, but Yours, be done" (Luke 22:42). Jesus surrendered to God's will. When we surrender to God's will instead of insisting on our own, we find peace and overcome our frustrations. Remember, Jesus taught us to pray, "Your will be done on earth as it is in Heaven" (Matthew 6:10). We need to have the right motivation. We all need the godly attitude of giving rather than receiving. Scripture tells us, "It is more blessed to give than to receive" (Acts 20:35).

Patience is another strategy for overcoming frustration. Several characteristics of love, or charity, are mentioned in 1 Corinthians 13, which is often called the "love chapter" in your Bible. What is the first characteristic? "Love suffers long and is kind" (1 Corinthians 13:4). Or, as the NIV states it, "Love is patient, love is kind". The Bible emphasizes our need for faith. Perhaps you are lacking faith and confidence. Can you have faith in this faithless age? Yes, you can. How? "So then faith comes by hearing, and hearing by the word of God" (Romans 10:17). Is it any wonder that many of us lack faith? If our priorities are materialistic, we will not have faith. Jesus of Nazareth made plain what our top priority in life should be. He addressed the common problem many have of worrying about their physical needs.

"Therefore I say to you, do not worry about your life, what you will eat or what you will drink; nor about your body, what you will put on. Is not life more than food and the body more than clothing? Look at the birds of the air,   for they neither sow nor reap nor gather into barns; yet your heavenly Father feeds them. Are you not of more value than they? Which of you by worrying   can add one cubit to his stature? So why do you worry about clothing? Consider the lilies of the field, how they grow: they neither toil nor spin; and   yet I say to you that even Solomon in all his glory was not arrayed like one of these. Now if God so clothes the grass of the field, which today is, and

tomorrow is thrown into the oven, will He not much more clothe you, *O ye of   little faith?* Therefore *do not worry*, saying, 'What shall we eat?' or 'What shall   we drink?' or 'What shall we wear?' For after all these things the Gentiles seek. For your heavenly Father knows that you need all these things. But   seek first the kingdom of God and His righteousness, and all these things
shall be added to you. Therefore do not worry about tomorrow, for tomorrow   will worry about its own things. Sufficient for the day is its own trouble" (Matthew 6:25–34).

Jesus encourages us to not be anxious or worry about our physical needs. The opposite of worry and anxiety is faith. So Jesus instructs us to focus on the spiritual. If we do, then all our physical needs will be added to us. Abraham obeyed God in faith. You need to decide whether you will step out in faith and obey God, or not. Abraham believed God's promises. Notice Paul's description of Abraham: "He did not waver at the promise of God through unbelief, but was strengthened in faith, giving glory to God, and being fully convinced that what He had promised He was also able to perform. And therefore "it was accounted to him for righteousness" (Romans 4:20–22). Ask yourself, "When I read about all of God's Promises in the Bible, do I really believe that He is able to perform everything He has promised"? If you do, you are well on your way to living by faith. Read your Bible and claim God's promises. He wants you to have a close relationship with Him. God promises to provide our every need. The Apostle Paul wrote, "And my God shall supply all your need according to His riches in glory by Christ Jesus" (Philippians 4:19). That is God's promise to you. Once you know God's promises, you can talk it over with God in prayer. You can claim God's promises. You will follow His instruction, "Ask, and it will be given to you; seek, and you will find; knock, and it will be opened to you. For everyone who asks receives, and he who seeks finds, and to him who knocks it will be opened" (Matthew 7:7–8). Take God at His word. Pray to Him, according to His will. Ask, seek, and knock. You will find that answered prayer will help you overcome your worries, frustrations, and anxieties with faith.

The godly qualities of patience, faith, obedience and surrender to God's will (and His divine love) will help us overcome our frustrations, fears and anxieties. God wants us to live by faith. He will give us that faith, if we draw close to Him in prayer, and seek to understand His will from the Bible. The Bible instructs us to pray daily. If we will humble ourselves to seek God in prayer, and if we read the Bible seeking to do God's will, He will give us more faith and more peace of mind. As the Apostle Paul wrote, "faith comes by hearing, and hearing by the word of God" (Romans 10:17). Three times in the New Testament, we read that "the just shall live by faith" (Romans 1:17; Galatians 3:11; Hebrews 10:38). As we draw closer to God in our actions and in our prayers, we can have the godly fear that will help us face our frustrations and experience the benefits of faith. God gives us amazing promises in His word, the Bible. We need to act on those promises. Then we can have the love that casts out fear and frustration, and we can live by faith.

Frustration also happens, when we're trying to do something in our own strength that we cannot do. It is a work of the flesh because we're trying to make something happen that only God can do through His grace. My personal definition of grace is God's power made available to us free of charge, enabling us to do with ease what we could never do on our own with any amount of struggle or effort. We all need the grace of God so when He calls us to something, we'll be equipped to do it. God's grace is amazing, but sometimes I wonder if we have forgotten how truly amazing it is. The word "grace" is often so common in church or other religious settings that it can become familiar, causing us to forget its true value. Romans 5:8 (AMP) says, "But God shows and clearly proves His [own] love for us by the fact that while we were still sinners, Christ (the Messiah, the Anointed One) died for us". God sent His Son to die for us before we were even following Him, which is amazing! I believe that when we have a true revelation of all God has done for us, we can overcome any frustration in our lives. God is not just with us but in us, and He will do through us what needs to be done when we stop trying to do it ourselves and let Him work. Ephesians 2:8 says, "For it is by free grace (God's unmerited favor) that you are saved (delivered from judgment and made partakers of Christ's salvation) through [your] faith. And this [salvation] is not of yourselves [of your own doing, it came not through your own striving], but it is the gift of God" (AMP). We are saved by the grace of God through our faith in Him; our faith does not buy our salvation; it merely receives it. As Ephesians 2:8 says, salvation "is the gift of God". It is impossible to buy a free gift, and this can be hard for us to understand. Our flesh wants to earn and deserve this free gift and take credit for being worthy. Salvation is given to us freely, by God's grace, and the same way we receive Christ's salvation, is the same way we have to live – by grace. God gives us His forgiveness and grace daily; we just have to believe and receive it.

When God forgives your sins, it means all your sins: past, present and future. You do not have to be afraid of sin because God has taken care of the problem. Some may worry that if we don't fear sin, we will keep sinning on purpose, but that's not true. If you are truly born again and really have a relationship with God, there is a new nature inside of you. Second Corinthians 5:17 (AMP) says, "If any person is [ingrafted] in Christ (the Messiah) he is a new creation (a new creature altogether); the old [previous moral and spiritual condition] has passed away. Behold, the fresh and new has come!" No one is perfect, and we all make mistakes sometimes. But if the Holy Spirit is living in your spirit through salvation, you won't be comfortable with those mistakes because God's nature is at work in you. The devil would love for us to feel like God is mad at us for our mistakes, but the truth is God is love and we need to humbly accept His love and grace. When we humble ourselves before the Lord and understand that everything good in our lives is by His grace, we open ourselves up to His help. First Peter 5:5 says that "God sets Himself against the proud…[and He opposes, frustrates, and defeats them], but gives grace (favor, blessing) to the humble" (AMP). This scripture helped me see that when I'm frustrated, God is trying to show me that I need to humble myself and let Him help me. My prayer usually sounds something like this: "God, I am nothing without You and can do nothing without You. I need You. Please help me". The key is humility. The humble get the help, not the prideful. Whatever God calls you to do in life, He will equip you to do it. You will be able to fulfill His will for your life and live frustration-free as you humble yourself before Him and receive His amazing grace. And when you do, He will do amazing things through you!

I have learned that frustration is an emotion that can keep you from reaching your full potential in God. In order to elevate in God, we have to know the right decisions to make when frustration tries to steal our joy. Frustration can serve as a steering wheel in our lives, when being steered correctly can take us to our destiny, but when being steered incorrectly can take us to place of destruction, and sometimes there is no bouncing back from that place. I have watched many people get frustrated and completely quit on God. Does their quitting mean that they were never called by God, or does it mean they were never taught how to deal with frustration? Hopefully during this chapter, you will learn how to still flow in God and give Him everything while battling frustration. When I think about the effects of frustration, my mind quickly goes to Moses. Moses was a man that overcame so many detrimental obstacles in his life, he was born during a time when Pharaoh summoned

that all male babies be drowned in the river while saving

all female babies. Even though this was an act that

everyone in Egypt was supposed to abide by, Moses had

a mother that was willing to defy this order and take a

drastic step to save her baby son. Exodus 2:2-3 states:

> "And the woman conceived, an bare a son: and when she saw him that   he was a goodly child, she hid him three months. (3) And when she could not longer hide him, she took for him an ark of bushes, and daubed it with slime   and with pitch, and put the child therein; and she laid it in the flags by the   river's brink".

This scripture lets us know that Moses was

supposed to be killed at birth, but God intervened so that

he could live. Now many may say, if it wasn't for Moses'

mother, but when God has purpose for your life, He may

use an individual to assist in carrying out the act, but all

glory goes to God. So as many know, Moses grew up in

Pharaoh's house being raised by Pharaoh's daughter

(who ended up finding Moses at the riverbank).

Compassion immediately came upon her, and she knew

within her heart that she was going to keep this baby boy,

and as a result she named him Moses. Now, Moses grew up in Pharaoh's house, but one day (when Moses had reached adulthood) he witnessed an Egyptian "smiting" an Hebrew, whom Moses considered as his brethren since Moses too was a Hebrew so that day he made a very critical decision, he chose to stand up for his people and as a result Moses murdered the Egyptian. The Bible lets us know in Exodus 2:11-12:

> "And it came to pass in those days, when Moses was grown, that he went out unto his brethren, and looked on their burdens: and he spied an Egyptian smiting a Hebrew, one of his brethren. (12) And he looked this way and that way, and when he saw that there was no man, he slew the Egyptian, and hid him in the sand".

Now Moses is a murderer. This is why I love God so, because even in the midst of all Moses had been through, God still wanted to use him. God knew that He picked the right man, He was sure of His choice, but even in the midst of all of that, frustration still came in the midst.

I recall after the passing of Corey, (our only son), the enemy desired for me to become frustrated. I missed our son so bad, but I knew God's calling was still the same. I felt in my spirit there were certain things that I should have been doing, and according to me, I wasn't doing them. I became frustrated. I was still running revivals at other churches, but I was still frustrated. Then I came to the point where I stopped attending church. I continued to pray, I continued to worship God, but I just did it in the comforts of my own home. I walked around like frustration was not getting the best of me, but in actuality it was. So even today, I am eternally grateful for the helpmeet that God gave. My wife did not say much to me, she kept going to church, but she knew in her spirit that something wasn't right. As only a wise woman would do, she summoned for help, she called some Pastors from Miami, that we normally fellowshipped with, and they came immediately. They did not ask me what I was thinking, they did not ask me what I was going through, the only thing they did was pray for me. When they began to pray, it seemed as if the house began to shake, and I could feel life coming back to me. I could feel the Holy Ghost renewing me, I can truly say I felt the hands of God. During that time, God gave me the command to start a church in Jasper, and He told me to name the church, Empowering Tabernacle House of Prayer Outreach Ministry Apostolic Faith. I went before my Pastor and my Church Mother, revealed what God had given me, received their blessings, and I was on my way to another chapter in my life. That was the first real encounter I had with that awful emotion frustration. The enemy strategically plans your demise. I had been hearing rumors throughout the community that since our only son was gone, our marriage wasn't going to last. People thought that both me and my wife was going to lose sight of God, they had everything planned out. In the midst of the rumors, the enemy added a heighten effect of frustration, and he thought that through that one act, all those rumors were going to be fulfilled. But I thank God for prayer, and I can truly say that what the enemy meant for my bad, God really turned it around for my good.

Moses continued through his journey doing some awesome things in God. He was at first hesitant on being used by God, because he felt his speech was not up to par, but God told Moses that it was okay, and gave him

his brother Aaron to speak for him. God also used Moses

to set those that was in bondage under the hands of

Pharaoh free. "God used Moses to lead the children of

Israel through the wilderness displaying all types of

miracles, when they were hungry God granted manna,

when they were thirsty Moses struck the rock and out

came water" (Lindsay: 44). God used Moses mightily, but

then one -day frustration took its toll on Moses. Moses

went up to have direct communication with God and to

receive keen instructions on how to continue to lead

God's people. The people began to get impatient, I can

see them in my spirit wondering what is taking Moses so

long, so they went to Aaron seeking another god. The

Bibles tells us in Exodus 32:1,

> "And when the people saw that
> Moses delayed to come down out of the
> mount, the people gathered themselves
> together unto Aaron, and said unto him, Up,
> make us gods, which shall go before us; for
> as for this Moses, the man that brought us
> up out of the land of Egypt, we **know** not
> what is become of him".

Instead of Aaron upholding the commands that God had given his brother, or even upholding the life he saw his brother live, Aaron gave in to the people. The Bible tells us that in verse two of the same chapter, *"And Aaron said unto them, Break off the golden earrings, which are in the ears of your wives, and sons, and of your daughters, and bring them unto me"* that Aaron began to help the people make idol gods to worship. Now when Moses came down, he probably was excited, he had a new word from God, and he also had tablets that had the law written on them that he could wait to share with the people. I can imagine in my spirit the excitement Moses must have felt on the inside. But when he saw the people, the Bible tells us in Exodus 32: 19, "And it came to pass, as soon as he came nigh unto the camp, that he saw the calf, and the dancing; and Moses' anger waxed hot, and he cast the tables out of his hands, and brake them beneath the mount". Moses' anger arose, and he became frustrated immediately. All he had done for the people, all the miracles they saw God demonstrate through Moses on their behalf, and when he had stepped away for an extended period of time, this is what they do. This lets me know how powerful frustration can become when fully manifested. Moses knew the importance of the tablets. He knew that they were strict instructions from God, but all that Moses knew was thrown out of the window as soon as frustration entered.

Think about in the ministry, God has done so much for all of us. We have witnessed miracle after miracle. God has been so good. Then something comes, and regardless of all God has done for us, frustration can cause us to act contrary to the things of God. It can cause us to lose sight of all that God has in store for us. As the body of Christ, and lovers of God, we must learn to shake things off instead of allowing it to frustrate us. Shake the devil off, even though all hell may be breaking loose around you, you must believe you can shake it off. It doesn't matter if the snake bit you, the swelling has arisen, and it seems as if it's hindering every move that you desire you make, shake it off. Even though the attack has happened on the outside (attacking our physical body), we must believe that we have enough on the inside to shake it off. Things that we see, and feel is contrary to the things of God, shake it off. Even when people all around us are losing focus, and we don't see the need to continue on, shake it off. If you do not shake it off, you will not get to what God has for you.

Moses was unable to shake some things off. He broke the tablets, but God being as merciful as He is, gave Moses words for a new tablet, but frustration came back again. God gave Moses specific instructions in Numbers 20:8 stating,

> "Take the rod, and gather thou the assembly together, thou, and Aaron thy brother, and speak ye unto the rock before their eyes; and it shall give forth his water, and thou shalt bring forth to them water out of the rock; so thou shall give the congregation and their beasts drink".

These were simple instructions that Moses was commanded to do. Now God had looked over so much of Moses frustration tactics and was willing to give him yet another chance. He simply asked him to take the rod, gather the assembly together, only speak unto the rock before their eyes, and then it shall give forth his water. Simple as that. The Bible lets us know that frustration would not allow Moses to obey the Words of the Lord,

Numbers 20:10-11 states,

> "And Moses and Aaron gathered the
> congregation together before the rock, and
> he said unto them, Hear now, ye rebels;
> must we fetch you water out of this rock?
> (11) And Moses lifted up his hand, and with
> his rod he smote the rock twice; and the
> water came out abundantly, and the
> congregation drank, and their beast also."

The punishment for this act of frustration was going to be so different from all the others. This one was going to affect Moses for the rest of his life. The Bible tells us that God was very displeased, and Numbers 20:12 lets us know, "And the Lord spake unto Moses, and Aaron, Because ye believed me not, to sanctify me in the eyes of the children of Israel, therefore ye shall not bring this congregation into the land which I have given them". God was not willing to just brush this one off so easily, but Moses had to pay for his act of disobedience and this payment was a harsh one. All that Moses did for the people, because his frustration caused him to act unseemly, he (nor his brother Aaron) would not be able to enter into the Promised Land that was promised to the children of Israel. I know that had to be heart breaking, crushing, to have done the majority of the work, but unable to reap the harvest. Frustration!

If we desire to be used by God and reach our destiny, we cannot allow frustration to cause us to lose out on everything. We cannot allow frustration to enter into our spirt and cause us to act contrary to the Word of God. Instead of allowing frustration to lead us, we must be willing to walk in God's Will – Dreams, Direction, and Destiny which is our assurance to be promoted from the least to the greatest. Allow these words of encouragement to push you to your greatest. Our life in Christ is a journey. The Bible says, "that young men shall have visions and old men shall dream of dreams" (Acts 2:17). Everywhere you go you write a story. Our life starts when we accept Jesus Christ as our personal Savior. We all have a starting point where we accept Jesus Christ, but there are no early retirements in the Lord. The only way your journey will end is death or Christ's coming. Dream your dreams in the will of God until they come to pass. Folks are looking for destiny in the wrong places. When you get in the will of God, He will teach you all things. We won't lose anything as long as were in the will of God, but we will lose everything out of God's will. It is a joy to be saved, it is a joy to have good children, and it is a joy to have peace – Life is Beautiful; it is a joy to have life. Override all your troubles and live your life. The joy that you have does not come from the world; it comes from God. God will provide you with the strength and you must do the work. For example: the shoestrings in my boots will not tie themselves. God has provided me with the strength to put on the shoes and to also tie them up. Therefore, let God do the 95% and you do the 5%. Something is wrong when people cannot be happy about the goodness of God because the peace of God surpasses all understanding. Make a joyful noise unto the Lord. People are in prison in their minds; come out of prison. The devil will have you walking around thinking that people don't like you, when in reality that is not the truth. You are a prisoner in your own mind. – Get out of prison! You have to deny your flesh in order not to rob

God and to get to the place where He wants you to be. The devil has captured your mind and put you in prison. But Jesus has already paid the price. Therefore, why do you have to be sick when Jesus is a healer? Destiny is short for destination. All over this nation, your name ought to mean something. You ought to be known everywhere you go because of God. As you walk with the Lord, there are three different levels in God: (1) A level of living – the enemy says that you cannot live above measure; you ought to live above what the enemy says, (2) A level of Achieving – you can achieve with God but without God, you can't do anything. Achieve by putting the 'super' on the natural and (3) A Level of Moving – to what God has for you; move from Grace to Grace and from Righteous to Righteous. Move up and move on because you are on a different level. In looking at the life of Christians, some people stay at a certain level for a long time. They get in different areas and don't know that there are guidelines to follow. They think that by using any means to get what they want it's okay, but it is not okay. There are guidelines to follow. There are four things that you need on your Christian journey in order to

Dream, Have Direction, and Destiny:

- **Dreams** – Our journey with God has to be according to the Word of God – The word of God will keep your life on course. Just like Jesus did everything in His Father, so must we. Jesus did not change His strategy and we should not change ours. Speak the word back to the devil, resist him, and he will flee (Matthew 4:3-10).

- **Direction** – Our journey with God; we must follow the Holy Spirit (the Leader). That's direction. We need direction; we cannot make it on our own. Jesus will not speak of Himself but He will speak of things that are sure to come. He will give, announce, and declare the things that the Father gives Him unto you. If you accept it, you will live. But if you reject it, you will die spiritually (not physically). He will take us some places that we would never be able to go on our own; learn some direction. We all have routines and the Holy Spirit wants to be our direction (John 16:12-13).

- **Destiny** – Our journey with God is accomplished by Faith. For without Faith, it is impossible to please God. If you seek Him; He will reward you openly. There are some things that we must turn down in order to save our house (family). People would rather run from responsibility than change. Live right and you will be blessed. Thank God for His Spirit and thank God for dreams, direction, and destiny (Hebrews 11:6-8).

Last but not least, our journey with God should be according to the nine fruits of the Spirit. When God speaks to you to do something, there is a battle between your head and your heart. Your head will look at your heart and give you every reason not to do what God has commanded you to do. Fear and frustration will paralyze you and keep you from advancing in the things of God. But stop looking at your natural circumstances. When you do what you want to do instead of obeying what God has told you to do, the nine fruits of the spirit will not be evident in your life. Stay in the center of God's will and walk in your destiny. If frustration has been hindering you from receiving, tell frustration today – NO MORE!

CHAPTER 9

GET IN TOUCH WITH THE NEW MAN

The new creation is described in 2 Corinthians 5:17: "Therefore, if anyone is in Christ, he is a new creation; the old has gone, the new has come"! The word "therefore" refers us back to verses 14-16 where Paul tells us that all believers have died with Christ and no longer live for themselves. Our lives are no longer worldly; they are now spiritual. Our "death" is that of the old sin nature which was nailed to the cross with Christ. It was buried with Him, and just as He was raised up by the Father, so are we raised up to "walk in newness of life" (Romans 6:4). That new person that was raised up is what Paul refers to in 2 Corinthians 5:17 as the "new creation". To understand the new creation, first we must grasp that it is in fact a creation, something created by God. John 1:13 tells us that this new birth was brought about by the will of God. We did not inherit the new nature, nor did we decide to re-create ourselves anew, nor did God simply clean up our old nature; He created something entirely fresh and unique. The new creation is completely new, brought about from nothing, just as the whole universe was created by God from nothing. Only the Creator could accomplish such a feat. Second, "old things have passed away". The "old" refers to everything that is part of our old nature – natural pride, love of sin, reliance on works, and our former opinions, habits, and passions. Most significantly, what we loved has passed away, especially the supreme love of self and with-it self-righteousness, self-promotion, and self-justification. The new creature looks outwardly toward Christ instead of inwardly toward self. The old things died, nailed to the cross with our sin nature.

The old has passed away, and the new has come! Old, dead things are replaced with new things, full of life and the glory of God. The newborn soul delights in the things of God and abhors the things of the world and the flesh. Our purposes, feelings, desires, and understandings are fresh and different. We see the world differently. The Bible seems to be a new book, and though we may have read it before, there is a beauty about it which we never saw before, and which we wonder at not having perceived. The whole face of nature seems to us to be changed, and we seem to be in a new world. The heavens and the earth are filled with new wonders, and all things seem now to speak forth the praise of God. There are new feelings toward all people – a new kind of love toward family and friends, a new compassion never before felt for enemies, and a new love for all mankind. The things we once loved, we now detest. The sin we once held onto, we now desire to put away forever. We "put off the old man with his deeds" (Colossians 3:9), and put on the "new self, created to be like God in true righteousness and holiness" (Ephesians 4:24). What about the Christian who continues to sin? There is a difference between continuing to sin and continuing to live in sin. No one reaches sinless perfection in this life, but the redeemed Christian is being sanctified (made holy) day by day, sinning less and hating it more each time he fails. Yes, we still sin, but unwillingly and less and less frequently as we mature. Our new self-hates the sin that still has a hold on us. The difference is that the new creation is no longer a slave to sin, as we formerly were. We are now freed from sin, and it no longer has power over us (Romans 6:6-7). Now we are empowered by and for righteousness. We now have the choice to "let sin reign" or to count ourselves "dead to sin but alive to God in Christ Jesus" (Romans 6:11-12). Best of all, now we have the power to choose the latter.

The Christian life is supposed to be a life lived by faith. It is by faith that we enter into the Christian life, and it is by faith that we live it out. When we begin the Christian life by coming to Christ for forgiveness of sin, we understand that what we seek cannot be obtained by any other means than by faith. We cannot work our way to heaven because nothing we could ever do would be sufficient. Those who believe they can attain eternal life by keeping rules and regulations—a list of do's and don'ts—deny what the

Bible clearly teaches. "But that no one is justified by the Law in the sight of God is clear, for, 'The just shall live by faith' (Galatians 3:11). The Pharisees of Jesus' day rejected Christ because He told them this very truth that all their righteous deeds were worthless and that only faith in their Messiah would save them.

In Romans 1, Paul says that the gospel of Jesus Christ is the power that saves us, the gospel being the good news that all who believe in Him will have eternal life. When we enter into the Christian life by faith in this good news, we see our faith grow as we come to know more and more about the God who saved us. The gospel of Christ actually reveals God to us as we live to grow closer to Him each day. Romans 1:17 says, "For in the gospel a righteousness from God is revealed, a righteousness that is by faith from first to last, just as it is written: "The righteous will live by faith". So, part of the Christian life is diligent reading and study of the Word, accompanied by prayer for understanding and wisdom and for a closer, more intimate relationship with God through the Holy Spirit.

The Christian life is also supposed to be one of death to self in order to live a life by faith. Paul told the Galatians, "I have been crucified with Christ and I no longer live, but Christ lives in me. The life I live in the body, I live by faith in the Son of God, who loved me and gave himself for me" (Galatians 2:20). Being crucified with Christ means that our old nature has been nailed to the cross and has been replaced by a new nature which is Christ's (2 Corinthians 5:17). He who loved us and died for us now lives in us, and the life we live is by faith in Him. It means sacrificing our own desires, ambitions, and glories and replacing them with those of Christ. We can only do this by His power through the faith that He gives us by His grace. Part of the Christian life is praying to that end. The Christian life is also supposed to persevere to the end. Hebrews 10:38-39 addresses this issue by quoting from the Old Testament prophet Habukkuk: "Now the just shall live by faith; But if anyone draws back, My soul has no pleasure in him". God is not pleased with one who "draws back" from Him after making a commitment, but those who live by faith will never draw back, because they are kept by the Holy Spirit who assures us that we will continue with Christ until the end (Ephesians 1:13-14). The writer of Hebrews goes on to verify this truth in verse 39: "But we are not of those who draw back to perdition, but of those who believe to the saving of the soul". The true Believer is one who believes until the end. So, the Christian life is one lived by faith in the God who saved us, empowers us, seals us for Heaven, and by whose power we are kept forever. The day-to-day life of faith is one that grows and strengthens as we seek God in His Word and through prayer and as we unite with other Christians whose goal to be Christ like is similar to our own. The new creation is a wondrous thing, formed in the mind of God and created by His power and for His glory. Jesus said that to become a Christian we must be "born again" (John 3:3). That phrase implies that we cannot simply remodel our current lives; we must start over. Corinthians

5:15 and 17 explain what happens when we put our trust in Jesus as Savior and Lord: "And He died for all, so that they who live might no longer live for themselves, but for Him who died and rose again on their behalf. . . Therefore, if anyone is in Christ, he is a new creature; the old things passed away; behold, new things have come". Jesus used the illustration of birth because we understand that when a baby is born, a new creation is evident. Live birth is followed by a transformation over time from infancy to maturity. When we are born again in the spirit, we who were "dead in trespasses and sins" (Ephesians 2:1, ESV; Romans 6:18) are brought to life. We are "created anew in Christ Jesus" (Ephesians 2:10). God changes our desires, outlook, and focus as we turn from self-worship to God-worship. Many people try to bypass this transfer of ownership and instead try to "clean up their act," "turn over a new leaf," or start going to church in an effort to feel like a Christian. However, willpower can only take us so far. Jesus did not come to reform our sinful flesh; He came to kill it (Luke

9:23; Romans 6:6–7). The old and new natures cannot work together, nor can they peacefully coexist (Romans 8:12–14). The flesh must die before we can experience the new life Jesus offers us (2 Corinthians 5:21). Every human being is composed of body, soul, and spirit (1 Thessalonians 5:23). Before we have a relationship with God through new birth, we live primarily controlled by our soul and body. The spirit lies dormant inside us, like a deflated balloon. When we transfer ownership of our lives to the lordship of Jesus Christ, He sends His Holy Spirit to regenerate our deflated spirits. The Holy Spirit is compared to a wind (John 3:8, Acts 2:2). At salvation, He pours into our hearts and inflates the spirit inside us so that we can now communicate with God. Whereas, a person was formerly directed by the sin nature, he or she can now be directed by the Holy Spirit who works to transform us into the image of Christ (Romans 8:29). We are to present our bodies as a living sacrifice and to renew our minds so that we begin to think as God thinks (Romans 12:1–2). As we focus on knowing

God, reading His Word, and surrendering ourselves daily to the control of the Holy Spirit, our choices change. Our pastimes, priorities, and passions change. The fruit of the Holy Spirit (Galatians 5:22–23) becomes evident where there were once only the works of the flesh (Galatians 5:19–21). Experiencing the new birth is only the beginning. God continues to work in us to present to Himself a holy people on that day when we see Him face to face (Philippians 1:6, 2:13, 2 Corinthians 11:2, Ephesians 5:27).

In a number of ways, the preparation for invasion and the conflict that lay before Joshua and the people begins in this chapter. And it is significant that this preparation in chapter one proceeds out of God's communication. First, God speaks and commissions Joshua (Joshua 1:1-5) and then calls him to be strong and courageous (Joshua 1:6-9). In view of this word from God, Joshua speaks to the people and gives them instructions for preparing to cross the Jordan in three days (Joshua 1:10-15). This is followed by the response of the people which, of course, had its source in the Word of God (Joshua 1:16-18). God's revelation should always be followed by a response that is in keeping with His inspired Word.

> "Now it came about after the death of Moses the servant of the Lord that the Lord spoke to Joshua the son of Nun, Moses' servant, saying,
>
> "Moses My servant is dead; now therefore arise, cross this Jordan, you and all this people, to the land which I am giving to them, to the sons of Israel.
>
> Every place on which the sole of your foot treads, I have given it to you, just as I spoke to Moses. From the wilderness and this Lebanon, even as far as the great river, the river Euphrates, all the land of the Hittites, and as far as the Great Sea toward the setting of the sun, will be your territory. No man will be able to stand before you all the days of your life. Just as I have been with Moses, I will be with you; I will not fail you or forsake you" (Joshua 1:1-5).

The victory and possession of the land which follows is a direct result of the Word of God and of man, in this case Joshua, hearing and responding to His Word. This should illustrate for us that there is absolutely no victory or chance for us to experience the blessings of our new life in Christ apart from the Word of God. Whenever any believer begins to turn away from the Word through indifference or apathy for whatever reason, he is turning away from the Lord and into defeat. Joshua's commission comes only after the death of Moses. Why is this? Moses was the great lawgiver who represented the Law of Sinai, which demonstrates the Holiness of God and the sinful condition of man who stands separated from God (Romans 3:23). But the Law, though holy and good, could never give life or spirituality nor could it provide justification. It was instead a ministration of death that revealed man a sinner and in jail to sin (2 Corinthians 3:7; Romans 7:7; Galatians 3:19-22). Moses portrayed the law which cannot lead us into the saving and abundant life of Christ. It was only a tutor, a temporary servant who must pass away (Galatians 3:23). Though it did point to Christ in the tabernacle, priesthood, and sacrifices, it could not take away sin or provide deliverance from the flesh. Why? Because it was weak in that it was dependent upon man and his ability (Romans 8:3-4). The Law provided a righteous standard, but no power or grace for the flesh or indwelling sin (Romans 6:14; 8:3).

Thus, Moses had to pass from the scene before Joshua could be commissioned and given orders to take the people across Jordan and into the Promised Land. A further reason is seen in Joshua's name which so clearly reminds us that "*Yahweh* is Salvation" (www.gotquestions.org). As the Hebrew equivalent of Jesus, Joshua typifies the Lord Jesus and His saving life who provides us not only with redemption, but with the power we need to enter into the possession of our possessions in Christ. With the mention of the death of Moses, Joshua is then told, "Now therefore arise, cross this Jordan, you and all this people". By way of application for today, the words "Now therefore arise", (in view of the death of Moses and what he represented) teach us the truth that no man can live the Christian life by keeping a set of laws or taboos. While the Christian life involves obedience to the principles and imperatives of the Word, it is more. It is a life to be lived by faith in the power of God. We simply cannot live the Christian life in our own energy or by our own determination. The Christian life is not just being Mr. Nice or merely keeping a set of Christian principles and rules. It is a faith relationship with God to be lived out in the power of the Spirit and in the light of the Word. With the Words, "arise, cross this Jordan", the Lord is saying, "get out of the desert and move on into Canaan". God's will for the believer is never in the wilderness. It is in Canaan, the place of deliverance and conquest. "Arise, cross" by the parallel of New Testament truth says, "take up your armor, use your supernatural resources, stop trusting in yourself, trust me and move out". "You and all this people" illustrates that spirituality is not just for an elect few, but it is for all believers. The abundant, maturing Christian life is God's plan and will for every single believer. It is only limited by our lack of availability to His constant availability to us. Every believer is blessed with every spiritual blessing, is a priest of God with abundant grace available for every situation. We need to remember all Israel got out of Egypt the same way - by faith in God's Grace, and they would all cross over Jordan in exactly the same way, by faith in God's deliverance. The words, "to the land which I am giving you" and in verse

3, "every place on which ..."illustrates the truth of Ephesians 1:3 and Colossians 2:10. "I am giving you" and "I have given it to you" shows us God was then in the process of bringing to pass that which had been theirs all along. Joshua 2:9-11 reveals that the land had virtually been theirs for 40 years. It was just waiting to be possessed. And like that, from the moment of salvation, God has provided every believer with every spiritual blessing and provision. Of course, as this book makes perfectly clear, having title deed to the land (or our blessings in Christ) does not mean our lives will be without testing, conflict, struggles, and pressures. It indeed will, but since the battle is the Lord's, since God has done the most for us in Christ, with the testing and temptations comes God's deliverance through faith and the application of the Word.

In verse 5, Joshua is given the promise, "no man will be able to stand before you," but this promise is also a warning. While the land was theirs for the taking, it would not be taken without conflict or battle. And likewise, as the land of Canaan was full of fortified cities and enemies that needed to be driven out, so the Christian life is a life of conflict with enemies which must be overcome. Though the outcome is assured if we claim God's sufficiency and the saving life of Christ, we must still do battle and reckon with the fact of the enemy throughout this life. This is a wakeup call, a reality that must be faced: life is full of battles and conflicts. We are not in Eden nor are we in the millennial reign of Christ. Rather we wrestle with the flesh (indwelling sin), with the devil and supernatural powers of darkness, and a world system that is antagonistic to God, to His Word, and to godly living (Romans 7:15, Galatians 5:16, Ephesians 5:15-16; 6:10, 1 Peter 5:8-9). Nevertheless, the positive side is that these words, "no man will be able to stand before you ..." are also a promise of continued deliverance in battle after battle after battle. Because of the infinite sufficiency of the saving life of the Christ through His finished work on the cross, His triumphant presence at the right hand of God, our identification with Him in His death, resurrection, and session in heaven, and through His gift of the Holy Spirit, there is no enemy we can possibly face which the Lord (our Joshua) has not already conquered. Our need is to appropriate what He has already done for us through the wise faith-application of His Word.

Though still active and roaming about, Satan's power has been broken and we can resist his deceptions and attacks. Though the sin principle still dwells within, or the flesh is still active in our members, its power over us has been broken through our union with Christ in His death and resurrection. This means the victory of possessing our possessions is through the gift of the Holy Spirit (Romans 6 and 8) and the sanctifying power of a Word-filled life (John 17:17; Ephesians 5:18; Colossians 3:16). We all entertain the desire to live in an ideal world, where life moves along smoothly without problems or stress. In fact, we were created for such, and it is not wrong to long for that time which will come with the return of the Lord Jesus, our Joshua. But the doctrines of the apostasy of the last days, the evil nature of this day and time, plus the presence of our three enemies are constant reminders that such cannot be the case now any more than we can have lasting and true world peace without the return of the Lord. We must face the facts and be prepared to face life as it really is. In Christ we are super-conquerors and through His saving life we can overcome the individual battles of life, but we must be prepared to fight the good fight. We all like to rock along without anything upsetting our schedules or forcing us out of our comfort zones. When we attempt to get away from the struggle, God jars us back into reality through some unpleasant condition or experience and we are again faced with reality. After vacation we must go back to work and face that co-worker who is so hard to get along with. We are going along and then suddenly, there is a threat to our health or that of our spouse or child. Or we may face the death of a loved one which brings heartache, loneliness, along with new pressures and responsibilities. Such is your life and mine, but the words "no man will be able to stand before you all the days of your life" intrudes into our lives with two realities: a warning and promise.

The words, "just as I have been with Moses, I will be with you; I will not fail you or forsake you", call our attention to one of the great truths of the Bible. Israel would get into the land the same way they got out of Egypt. Likewise, we enter into the abundant life of Christ the same way we were delivered from wrath – by faith in the saving life of Christ. Just as we trusted in Christ and the accomplishments of the cross for justification and redemption, so we must reckon on those same accomplishments as the basis for our security and daily deliverance (Romans 6:4-11; Colossians 2:6-3:3).

> "Be strong and courageous, for you shall give this people possession of the land which I swore to their fathers to give them. Only be strong and very courageous; be careful to do according to all the law which Moses My servant commanded you; do not turn from it to the right or to the left, so that you may have success wherever you go. This book of the law shall not depart from your mouth, but you shall meditate on it day and night, so that you may be careful to do according to all that is written in it; for then you will make your way prosperous, and then you will have success. Have I not commanded you? Be strong and courageous! Do not tremble or be dismayed, for the Lord your God is with you wherever you go" (Joshua 1:6-9).

While the first five verses deal with Joshua's commission to take over after the death of Moses, the major thrust of verses 6-9 concerns something that was vital to Joshua's ability to do that. And what was true for Joshua is equally true for us. There is a word or theme repeated at least three times in these verses that we need to pick up on and relate to. Three times God tells Joshua, "Be strong and courageous" (Joshua 1:6, 7, 9). Then later, as it pertains to their obedience to God, Joshua will relate the same charge to the people (Joshua 1:18; 10:25) who will likewise face the challenges and fulfillment of God's purposes for the nation – dwelling in the land as a priesthood nation as God's representative to the nations. So, the issue before Joshua was a call to be strong and courageous in view of the mantle of leadership that was being passed on to him. God was calling him to a very special and difficult ministry, one with tremendous challenges and obstacles far beyond his own skill or abilities. But life for all of us is filled with such challenges so let us not pass over this without seeing the personal application this can have for each of us. Joshua verses 6-9, are fundamental for obtaining the strength and courage anyone needs for the challenges of any ministry or responsibility. This passage is not just for a special class of leaders like pastors or missionaries. God has called each of us to ministry. No Believer is exempt. We are all gifted, we are all priests of God, and leaders in some sense with personal responsibilities to others whether elders, deacons, moms, or dads, etc.

People often run from ministry or difficult situations because of fear or because of the obstacles. As the former generation of Israelites had failed to enter into the land and possess their possessions because of unbelief and fear of the giants, so we too can fail to enter into God's calling on our lives. Without God's strength and personal courage, we will fail to tackle the challenges or take on the responsibilities that God calls us to. Others, being overconfident in themselves may seek to strike out on their own, an equally wrong way to try to serve the Lord as we will see illustrated in chapter 7 of Joshua with the defeat at Ai. Biblically speaking, where does moral strength and courage come from, and does it mean the absence of fear? Moral strength and courage come from:

> (1) faith in the sovereignty and provision of God and

>> (2) in the fact that we are convinced what we are doing is right and best and essential to life. But there is much more as this passage will show us.

Courage is that quality of mind that enables men to encounter danger and difficulty with firmness and resolve in spite of inner fears (1 Corinthians 2:3; 2 Corinthians 7:5). In other words, courage is not the absence of fear. But not all men are courageous by nature as Joshua was, and that fact is both explicit and implicit in Scripture. The highest degree of courage is seen in the person who is most fearful but refuses to capitulate to it. However fearful they might have been, God's leaders in succeeding generations have been commanded to be of good courage. Had they been without fear, the command would have been pointless.

Knowing God's Word, the clearly revealed will of God, plus recognizing one's gifts, abilities, and training, all of which are a part of understanding His pleasure or will for one's life, is foundational for finding strength and courage to accept any area of responsibility in ministry. Without this understanding, one will hardly have the motivation or courage to move into the ministries God wants to call us to. There is a specific process to be noted here in the Book of Joshua verses 1-9. There is first God's Word to Joshua commissioning and encouraging him. The courage that is called for here is the direct result of the Word and knowing God's will (Ephesians5:9-10). Also, Joshua is reminded that he had been prepared and trained for this as the servant of Moses (1:1). Joshua being spoken to in verse 1 is equivalent to us gaining biblical insight. It is this that forms the foundation for courage and conviction and for faith and action. We need to pray and seek God's will and wisdom. The first foundation for courage is knowing both the Word and God's will. Being the understudy of Moses illustrates a couple of key principles:

(1) The principle of having a godly example (1 Timothy 4; 1 Peter 5:1-3).

 (2) The principle of Luke 16:10 and its impact on the development of courage and motivation for ministry.

Joshua had been faithful in the little things and would be faithful in much. Service in the larger areas of responsibility starts with faithfulness in smaller things. We each need to find a place to serve and grow. It may become the training ground for other areas of ministry to which God may be calling you. "Moses my servant is dead" (Joshua 1: 2). This statement reminds us that no one is indispensable and leadership changes. If we are not training others and being trained ourselves, we leave gaping holes (2 Timothy 2:2). "Now therefore arise" emphasizes the need for decision making to fill the void left by the absence of Moses. And this is true for all of us in ministry for whatever reason there is a void left by the removal of the servants of God. A true grasp of the need is always a vital element to decisiveness and action to fill that need; it is part of the root that produces the fruit. But there is another element that is vital to courage and decisiveness in doing the will of God. Please note the promises given to Joshua, were given in relation to the ministry and work to which God had called him. This applies to each of us regardless of the particular ministry God has called us to in the body of Christ. Read these verses carefully and see what application you can make from them to your life. Do you feel the tug of God on your life to serve him in a particular way, but you are afraid? Are you afraid of failure? Are you afraid of what it might cost you? Meditate on these verses. We might also note some of the obstacles that can be observed in this passage because in claiming the promises of God, we must face our obstacles with faith.

Crossing the Jordan.......in Scripture, the Jordan often represents an obstacle, an impediment to growth, ministry, and progress. There is good reason to believe that the Jordan was swollen over its banks at this time of year (Joshua 3:15; 4:18). Here is one of the reasons courage is needed. Further, to cross the Jordan meant to enter into a hostile land, a land full of enemies some of whom were giants and who lived in strongly fortified cities. This was no simple challenge. Remember, the previous generation failed at Kadesh Barnea because of a lack of courage. But there is more here. "You and all this people". Their very numbers made this a prodigious task. But Joshua had the responsibility of leading a people who were noted for being stiff necked and throwing stones at their leaders. The word "all" reminds us that it is God's purpose for all His people to mature and become strong, to be in His will and living victorious lives. Nevertheless, regardless of the obstacles, God's will had been clearly made known to Joshua. He needed to act on this fact by faith in the Lord's person, promises, and provision. Let us look at the promise in verse 2: "To the land which I am giving to them, to the sons of Israel". Also note the words "which I have given to them". They were going into the Promised Land, the land promised to the patriarchs, to Abraham, Isaac, and Jacob or Israel by God Himself who cannot go back on His promises. In fact, He was then and had for some time been preparing the inhabitants for defeat (Joshua 2:9). The land had been theirs for forty years, but they failed to enter in because of unbelief and a lack of courage. God's Word is filled with hundreds of promises (Joshua 3-6, 9). In essence, every principle of Scripture becomes a promise because with the principle comes the inherent promise of God who is perfect veracity so that we can count on the principle. But we must know those promises and act on them by faith. God's promises are given to carry us through the Jordan Rivers of life, not necessarily to remove them but to enable us to step out in faith to cross them. They are not given so we can avoid or go around, but so we can cross them victoriously. How do we claim and act on those promises? How do we make those promises a part of our lives? Strength and courage come through daily Renewal in God's Principles (Joshua 1:7-8). Successful ministry according to a biblical definition of success is ultimately related to solid Bible teaching and study rather than to our human methods, techniques, and strategies which too often resort to pressure, coercion, and manipulation in order to achieve our own agendas or results. The Word is intrinsically powerful and able to produce godly change in believers' lives as it motivates, encourages, gives hope and direction, and exposes us to both our needs and God's provision. The Word has been given to us to establish a communicative relationship with God. It is a means of fellowship with Him. But this takes time, quality time and diligence. Note the emphasis on this in these verses. "To do according to all the Law...; do not turn from it", "but you shall meditate on it day and night").

What is our tendency? The average person today wants a quick fix—three easy steps. We want God to do it now. But this kind of approach does not develop a relationship with the Lord. Relationship with God, knowing Him, as with any relationship, takes time. It is this that provides us with success in ministry and in life, wherever we go and in whatever we do. Joshua was warned or cautioned in three things: To "be careful" warns against danger, calls for prudence, observation or careful scrutiny, and conscientiousness (Ephesians 5:15). To "do according to all" points to the concept of the whole counsel of the Word. To "not to turn from it" points to the concept of the Scripture as our objective index or standard and warns against moral relativity. Joshua was to do three things with regard to the Scriptures: The Law was not to depart from his mouth; he was to talk about it (Deuteronomy 6:7). This would be a means of staying occupied with God's thoughts and ways. He was to meditate on it day and night; he was to think about it constantly (Psalm 1:2; 119:97). In order to be able to talk about it and apply it, one must know it and see how it applies. We must have it on our mind and heart to fortify, encourage, and direct. He was to do everything written in it; he was to conduct his life in obedience to all its commands (Ezra 7:10; James 1:22-25).

Last, but certainly not least is the promise of the ever watchful and protective presence of God. There is no situation, no problem or enemy that we ever face alone. The Lord is always there as our constant support and supply. If we are concerned about our ministries or anything else, we can be absolutely sure God is infinitely more concerned than we are. Our need is simply to walk in the light of His presence and to count on His guidance, support, supply, and care by keeping our focus on Him (Hebrews 12:1-2).

"Have I not commanded you?" What is the important point here? It is the source of the command and the promises. The 'I' refers to God. "For the Lord, your God is with you wherever you go" (Joshua 1:9). These words stress the nature of the one who gave the command. They focus our attention on who and what God is like. One of the secrets to boldness and courage is an awareness of God's provision and presence, especially His presence as the one who has promised to never leave us. Compare John 20:19 and the fear of the disciples before they experienced the presence of the resurrected Christ with the promise of His never-ending presence (Matthew 28:18-20) with the boldness they displayed in Acts 4:13-20. What made the difference in the disciples? These were men who were now confident of Christ's presence (Matthew 28:18-20), knew God's will, His word, and who were filled with God's Spirit (Acts 4:8). When the Holy Spirit is in control of a man's life and is instructing him in God's Word, He imparts not "a spirit of timidity, but of power and love and discipline......For God has not given us a spirit of timidity, but of power and love and discipline" (2 Timothy 1:7).

In Hebrews13:1-3, the author reminded his readers of the need of ministry to the saints. For instance, he wrote, "let love of the brethren continue. Do not neglect to show hospitality to strangers, ..." God wants us to be ministering people and this takes courage and obedience, and sometimes means sacrifices. So also, he cautions us concerning our values and our sources of security and then reminds us of the promise of the presence and supply of God. Let your character be free from the love of money, being content with what you have; for He Himself has said, "I will never desert you, nor will I ever forsake you," so that we confidently say, "The Lord is my helper, I will not be afraid. What shall man do to me"? (Hebrews 13:5-6) As we face the challenges and opportunities and calling of God, let us remember these promises of God to Joshua. With the call of God to service there is always the matching provision of God. The problem lies not with the Lord, but with our responsibility to follow the Lord's admonitions as given to Joshua. Then Joshua commanded the officers of the people, saying, "Pass through the midst of the camp and command the people, saying, "Prepare provisions for yourselves, for within three days you are to cross this Jordan, to go in to possess the land which the Lord your God is giving you, to possess it" (Joshua 1:11).

"And to the Reubenites and to the Gadites and to the half-tribe of Manasseh, Joshua said, "Remember the word which Moses the servant of the Lord commanded you, saying, 'The Lord your God gives you rest, and will give you this land.' Your wives, your little ones, and your cattle shall remain in the land which Moses gave you beyond the Jordan, but you shall cross before your brothers in battle array, all your valiant warriors, and shall help them, until the Lord gives your brothers rest, as He gives you, and they also possess the land which the Lord your God is giving them. Then you shall return to your own land, and possess that which Moses the servant of the Lord gave you beyond the Jordan toward the sunrise" (Joshua 1:12-15).

In our previous lesson, the key note was God's revelation to Joshua concerning His promises, His purposes for the nation, the great principles of the Law, and His abiding presence. This forms the backdrop, the motivation and inspiration for this section and all that follows. Now, in verses 10-15, Joshua speaks to the people to act on the revelation and promises of God. Here the keynote is Joshua's immediate and obedient response regardless of the obstacles that lay before them. There is in this section a note of urgency, certainty, expectancy, and faith in Joshua's commands to the people. As God had commanded the new leader was taking charge and following the Lord's orders with confidence.

> (1) He did so immediately, without delay or procrastination. There is an old adage, "strike while the iron is hot". The longer we delay, the more reluctant we are to comply with God's requirements. Delay is dangerous to our spiritual lives and can lead to hardening against God's directives. Delay can also be disobedience. Procrastination can evidence a lack of heart for God's call and a lack of concern for God's glory and God's people. Note Psalm 119:60, "I hastened and did not delay to keep Thy commandments".

(2) He did so with confidence showing faith in the Lord and courage to tackle the task that lay before him. Such immediate response shows faith in the Word and confidence in the Lord.

(3) He did so with a clear understanding of what they faced. This brings out the element of his courage even more. First, by his own experience he understood what they faced, for forty years earlier he was one of twelve spies who had had been sent to search out the land. He could have remembered with pessimism the negative report of the ten and anticipated the same kind of response from the new generation. But Joshua's eyes were solidly on the Lord. Too often we undermine our focus on the Lord and His power by thinking about all the negatives, about what might happen if we move forward. Second, Joshua may have also known what they were facing through the report of the two spies he sent into the land in chapter 2, which probably occurred before the command of verse 11. Regardless, Joshua and the people faced a situation that in many ways paralleled the dilemma Moses and the Israelites had faced at the Red Sea (Exodus 14). "In each case, the obstacle occurred at the beginning of the leader's ministry. Both were impossible to solve through natural means. Both demanded implicit and absolute dependence upon a miracle-working God." After forty years of wandering, thinking they had at last come to the Promised Land, they find the river overflowing its banks (3:15). They faced what was for them an insurmountable difficulty. Life is like that isn't it? So often when our hopes are high, when things

seem to be going our way, suddenly, problems loom up out of nowhere and we seem to be looking at an impossible crossing. But all things are possible for God who works all things together for those who love Him (Genesis 18:14; Jeremiah 32:17; Matthew19:26; Luke 1:37; 18:27) (biblescripture.net/NIV).

Two matters had to be taken care of before they could cross the Jordan. Later, in 3:1 Joshua will give specifics on how the Jordan must be crossed, but first, as a good leader, he responsibly surveys the situation and sees two things that need to be done. The food gathered here is that which had been taken as spoils of their conquests through the wilderness. The manna was still available, but it could not be kept overnight without spoiling. They would be on the march moving from Shittim to the banks of the Jordan, which was only about eight miles, but because of the number of people and all that was involved, they evidently would not be able to gather the manna. The issue here is sustenance in order to be able to cross over and possess their possessions and handle the battles they would face by faith in the Lord's power. So likewise, we need to be nourished on the Words of the faith so we can continue to enter into our blessings in Christ (1 Timothy 4: 6 and Hebrews 3:7-19). In verses 12-14, Joshua reminds the tribes of Gad, Reuben, and the half tribe of Manasseh of their previous promises and responsibilities (Numbers 32:16-32; Deuteronomy 3:12-20). In this, we see a key to Joshua's success.

> (1) He was obeying his commission to "be careful to do according to all the law of Moses."He was remembering and seeking to live by the principles and promises of the Word. Compare 1:13, "Remember the word which Moses ... commanded you". This had become the Word for Israel.

> (2) He reminded the people of the Word. His authority for his challenge to these two-and-a-half tribes was the Word of the Lord. "This was no natural prudence or a spirit of expediency which actuated Joshua to seek their co-operation." And it was not merely a matter of seeking more help because they would be insufficient without more resources. It was not asking this as a favor to himself. No, the appeal and authority came from the facts of the commands of the Word of God. Servants of God must learn to lean on the power of the Word to motivate and minister to others and to accomplish God's purposes (biblescripture.net/NIV).

In principle however, this directive from Moses, enacted by Joshua was promoting the concept of the people of God as team. Here he was delegating specific tasks to these people. Each person was needed, and each needed to do his part. They would act as shock troops going before their brothers. There is also here another factor. In the words of verse 13, "The Lord your God gives you rest, and will give you this land" followed by the words of verse 15, "until the Lord gives your brothers rest, as He gives you, ..." Joshua was reminding them of their obligation to their people and placing an additional obligation on them based on gratitude for what God had already done for them. And they answered Joshua, saying, "All that you have commanded us we will do, and wherever you send us we will go. Just as we obeyed Moses in all things, so we will obey you; only may the Lord your God be with you, as He was with Moses. Anyone who rebels against your command and does not obey your words in all that you command him, shall be put to death; only be strong and courageous." In any successful enterprise of God's people, the leaders must have the support of the people if the work is going to fly. We might title this section, Joshua's Encouragement. He had honored God's Word and now God was honoring Joshua by moving the people to respond. It is tremendously encouraging to leaders and people alike when people respond to the Word with obedience and commitment. By the same token, it can be discouraging to see the opposite. In such times, both the leaders and the people must continue to trust the Lord, examine their ministries, and look to the Lord to move them to obedience rather than resort to some form of manipulation or coercion. The people were not only willing to obey, but they were willing to deal with any disobedience in their midst because of the demoralizing effect on others and the dishonor it brings to the Lord. This is always crucial for any people of God. This illustrates the need for the careful and loving application of church discipline in the body. Such is never easy. It requires real commitment and must always be done with a view to reconciliation and to recover a sinning Believer.

The statement, "only may the Lord your God be with you, as He was with Moses," can be taken in two ways. It may be taken as a condition or as a wish or prayer. If it is taken as a condition, they were saying they wanted to see clear evidence that Joshua was being led of the Lord, that he was truly God's man walking with the Lord. If it is taken as a prayer or wish, it demonstrated their recognition of this need if they were to be successful. It stated the fact they recognized they were all insufficient for the task, but that the Lord was sufficient. They needed a leader who was in touch with the living God. In this we see the need for God's leaders to be examples to the flock (Hebrews 13:7). People need and want to see mature spiritual reality in their leaders. It was because of this that Paul encouraged Timothy with the following words:

1 Timothy 4:11-16. Teach these things. Let no one look down on your youthfulness, but rather in speech, conduct, love, faith and purity, show yourself an example of those who believe. Until I come, give attention to the public reading of Scripture, to exhortation

and teaching. Do not neglect the spiritual gift within you, which was bestowed upon you through prophetic utterance with the laying on of hands by the presbytery. Take pains with these things; be absorbed in them, so that your progress may be evident to all. Pay close attention to yourself and to your teaching; persevere in these things; for as you do this you will ensure salvation both for yourself and for those who hear you.

Humanly speaking, how difficult was the task that confronted Joshua and the people with regard to entering the land of Canaan? What were some of the obstacles Joshua and the people faced? As the leader, Joshua faced following in the steps of a leader like Moses and leading a stubborn, stiff-necked group of people. All of them together faced fortified cities, giants, and a flooded Jordan. Everything Joshua and the people were called to do, humanly speaking, was far beyond their ability. From the crossing of the swollen and turbulent waters of the Jordan to conquering the fierce, powerful, ungodly people who occupied the land. Regardless of these obstacles, by believing the promises of

God, by applying the principles of God's Word, and by counting on the presence of God's person, Joshua courageously moved ahead and secretly sent two men to spy out the land to gather needed strategic and tactical information that any military commander would need to plan a successful strategy for taking the land. Then Joshua the son of Nun sent two men as spies secretly from Shittim, saying, "Go, view the land, especially Jericho." We might wonder, why Joshua sent out the spies. Was this necessary if he was really trusting in the Lord? After all, had not God promised Joshua that He would give him success? Why didn't he just go-ahead knowing God would somehow supply? After all, the battle is the Lord's … isn't it? Joshua had the precedent of the leadership and example of Moses for this action, an action which was the result of God's own command in Numbers 13:1-2. By application, Joshua was living and acting on the precepts of Scripture as he was commanded to do early on. While Joshua had the promise of God's deliverance, he had not been given instruction on just how God would defeat the enemies they would face. As a wise military leader, he was simply gathering information concerning the layout of the enemies' defenses, the condition of their moral, and other factors that would be important to any military campaign. Moreover, he was not to presume on the Lord. He was to trust the Lord implicitly, but in that trust, he was also to use the resources God gave him: the training, the men, and the wisdom he had gained. (Matthew 4:6-7) Faith in the Lord's provision should never lead to presuming on God's decrees or sovereign actions, our intuitive feelings, or on our wants and desires. Faith looks for the principles of Scripture that might be applicable, gathers information or the facts needed in making wise decisions, and then, based on biblical principles and the facts known, moves ahead trusting in the provision and directions of the Lord (Luke 14:31). If the Lord wants to intervene in some miraculous way as with Jericho, that is great, but we should never presume on His sovereign ways. Why the secrecy? Obviously, the spies were to go into the land secretly, as spies do. Here, the reference to secrecy had to do with the people of Israel. He did not inform them that he was sending in the spies. Nehemiah did similarly when he surveyed Jerusalem. Joshua was acting on behalf of God's purposes and in the peoples' best interests. He remembered the evil report of the spies from the preceding generation and the way this disheartened the people. People are people and he didn't want them to unnecessarily get their eyes on the problems. Sometimes it is wise for the leaders to do what is needed to keep the eyes of their people on the Lord and His promises rather than on the problems. The need is to encourage one another. We sometimes have to face the problems, but we must learn to do so through the eyes of faith in God's person, promises, principles, and purposes. This was a matter of discretion and God's leading through studying and knowing what was best in this particular situation. Sometimes it is good to call everyone's attention to the problems, other times it is not (Nehemiah 2:4-17). Note the text says, "especially Jericho" which shows us Joshua was particularly interested in this city. Why? Jericho lay just five miles on the other side of the Jordan and was one of the most formidable fortresses in the land. Conquering this city would not only give them a strong foothold into the land, but conquering Jericho would literally split the forces of the Canaanites by coming into Canaan in the middle hindering their communication and supply lines. This would have a further demoralizing effect on the rest of the inhabitants. Again, this illustrates how after praying for wisdom (James 1:5), we all need to assess and evaluate our own situations: Where we are, where we need to go, God's calling on our lives, our gifts and talents, our weaknesses, hindrances, and the circumstances and forces we are facing. Then, based on this information, establish plans, goals and objectives along with priorities and attack the problem accordingly, all the while resting in God's intervention and direction (Proverbs 16:1). Start with the things that are the most important and work on them one by one. This includes our personal life (spiritual needs, physical needs, and educational needs), our family life (relationships, spiritual needs, etc. as a family), our church life and personal calling and so on. So, they went and came into the house of a harlot whose name was Rahab and lodged there. Rahab is mentioned eight times in Scripture (Joshua 2:1, 3; 6:17, 23, 25; Matthew 1:5; Hebrews 11:31; James 2:25), and in six of these occurrences, her name is found with a specific descriptive noun. Do you know what it is? It is "harlot." Why did the men go in to a harlot? Is there anything we can learn from this?

This has created problems for many. To remove this stigma because her name is listed among the ancestors of the Savior in Matthew 1:5, it has even been argued that she was not a harlot but was only an 'innkeeper. One expositor, Arthur W. Pink, admits that she had been a harlot, but you can tell it bothers him. He says, "They were divinely directed to that particular house, though it is not likely they were personally conscious of the fact at the first" (bible.org). Then a few lines later he adds: "The house in which they sheltered was owned by a harlot, named Rahab: not that she was still plying her evil trade, but that formerly she had been a woman of ill fame, the stigma of which still clung to her" (bible.org).

Unless Arthur W. Pink is assuming from Joshua 2:9 and Rahab's statement of faith included an understanding of the Law and its statutes, I see no scriptural support for this, only a prejudice that God could and would use such a woman or draw her to Himself while she was still working as a harlot. It's almost as though she had to clean up her act before she could get saved or before God could work in her heart. "Josephus sought to clear the spies of any suspicion for having stayed at the house of a prostitute by calling Rahab an innkeeper" (bible.org). 'Innkeeper' and 'prostitute', however, were synonymous terms in that culture. Rahab's house was the only place where the men could stay with any hope of remaining undetected and where they would be able to gather the information they were seeking. Moreover, her house afforded an easy way of escape since it was located on the city wall. There is no indication that Rahab was a temple prostitute. More than likely, the two spies met her in the street where she could have been practicing her trade or perhaps, hearing of them, she was out looking for them as though she were drumming up customers as was the custom of a harlot or even an innkeeper (Proverbs 7:6-23). At this time, she had come to believe that Israel's God was the true God, but living in this totally decadent culture, it is unlikely she had such understanding of the Law of Moses. Rahab may have recognized the men as strangers, and because the whole city was on alert to the possibility of spies, and because of her convictions about the God of Israel, she may have concluded they were Israelites and invited them into her house for protection and to express her faith, but not for business.

This wonderfully illustrates God's Grace. He is no respecter of persons. He accepts and forgives us not because of what we are or might be, but because of His Son, because of what He would do and now has done and will do through those who trust Him and act in faith. It matters not what we were or have been. What matters is who Jesus Christ is, what He has done, and whether or not we will put our trust in Him. This also points to God's sovereign control over the affairs of men and how He directs the steps of those who rest in His provision or are looking to know Him better. God had worked in Rahab's heart, He knew her faith, her longing to know God and perhaps even to become a part of God's people, so God sovereignly worked and brought the spies and Rahab together for their protection and her blessing. God could have made the spies invisible or smote the people with blindness or used angels, but He chose to use two men and one woman walking by faith with courage to act on their convictions and He chose to use the more normal circumstances of life. In order for us to trust the Lord, are we looking for miracles, the sensational, and asking for out-of-the-ordinary experiences before we will step out and count for the Lord? Or are we willing to step out in the normal situations of life trusting God to use us and lead us to ordinary people whose hearts He has touched? Note that Joshua is an interesting combination of the miraculous and the ordinary. And it was told the king of Jericho, saying, "Behold, men from the sons of Israel have come here tonight to search out the land." And the king of Jericho sent word to Rahab, saying, "Bring out the men who have come to you, who have entered your house, for they have come to search out all the land" These verses indicate the whole city had been on alert and the spies were recognized and seen going into the home of Rahab. The fact the king did not tear down the door and storm into the house may have been a matter of oriental hospitality. They had great respect for hospitality even in this decadent city. In fact, Unger says, "Oriental custom accords an almost superstitious respect to a woman's apartment". The king would have assumed that the spies were staying with Rahab. In antiquity too, as in modern times, prostitutes frequently were involved in intelligence activities. The king expected Rahab to do her patriotic duty and turn the spies in. But the woman had taken the two men and hidden them, and she said, "Yes, the men came to me, but I did not know where they were from. And it came about when it was time to shut the gate, at dark that the men went out; I do not know where the men went. Pursue them quickly, for you will overtake them." But she had brought them up to the roof and hidden them in the stalks of flax which she had laid in order on the roof. So, the men pursued them on the road to the Jordan to the fords; and as soon as those who were pursuing them had gone out, they shut the gate. In these verses Rahab conceals the spies, lies to protect the soldiers, and sends the soldiers of the king on a wild goose chase. Because to do otherwise was an act of treason and punishable by death, the king believed her to be loyal and didn't even have her home searched. At this point, we would do well to look at two New Testament verses and one Old Hebrews 11:31 by faith Rahab the harlot did not perish along with those who were disobedient, after she had welcomed the spies in peace. James 2:25 - And in the same way was not Rahab the harlot also justified by works, when she received the messengers and sent them out by another way? Joshua 6:17 And the city shall be under the ban, it and all that is in it belongs to the Lord; only Rahab the harlot and all who are with her in the house shall live, because she hid the messengers whom we sent. Why was Rahab saved? Because she had believed in the God of Israel. Hiding the messengers was an outworking of her faith. To hide the messengers was a calculated deception to protect them, just as many godly people hid Jews in European countries during World War II. First, what Rahab did was a matter of faith. She had come to believe that the God of Israel was indeed "God in heaven above and earth beneath" (Joshua 2:11) and she is listed in the faith Hall of Fame chapter. Second, Rahab's faith, which gave her strong convictions about God, caused her to act on her faith to the point of putting her life on the line. She knew eventually Israel would attack the city and destroy it because their God was the true God, and she wanted to be delivered and to become a part of Israel. She did not know a lot about Israel's God, His laws of righteousness, or the way of salvation, but she knew He was the supreme God. What about Rahab's lie? Was it justified? Does Scripture condone it? Most commentaries approve of her faith but disapprove of her lie. In essence, they approve of her hiding the spies, but not telling the lies. For instance: Dr. Campbell writes, "To excuse Rahab for indulging in a common practice is to condone what God condemns. ....The lie of Rahab was recorded but not approved. The Bible approves her faith, demonstrated by good works, but not her falsehood". Dr.

Unger writes, "Rahab's lie, of course was morally wrong"

(bible.org).

Arthur W. Pink agrees and says, "She failed to fully trust

the Lord, and the fear of man brought a snare. He whose

angels had smitten the men of Sodom with blindness

(Genesis 19:11) and who had slain the fifty men sent to

lay hands on His prophet (2 Kings 1:9-12), could have

prevented those officers finding the spies". But is this

correct? What was she supposed to say? "If you think

they are here, come on in and search the house". Please

note, this is a matter of warfare. In Joshua 6:17, Joshua

explains that Rahab was to be spared because she hid

the spies, and she did this as an ally. Let's be honest

here. When you take a vacation, do you leave a light on

or have the TV come on in the evening to give the

impression you are home when in truth, you are gone?

We do this to deceive intruders, but it's not the truth.

Deception is an important strategy in warfare. Espionage

would be impossible without it. When Rahab hid the

spies, she sided with Israel against her own people. It was an act of treason" (bible.org)!

> "Now before they lay down, she came up to them on the roof, and said to the men, I know that the Lord has given you the land, and that the terror of you has fallen on us, and that all the inhabitants of the land have melted away before you. For we have heard how the Lord dried up the water of the Red Sea before you when you came out of Egypt, and what you did to the two kings of the Amorites who were beyond the Jordan, to Sihon and Og, whom you utterly destroyed. And when we heard it, our hearts melted and no courage remained in any man any longer because of you; for the Lord your God, He is God in heaven above and on earth beneath. Now therefore, please swear to me by the Lord, since I have dealt kindly with you, that you also will deal kindly with my father's household, and give me a pledge of truth, and spare my father and my mother and my brothers and my sisters, with all who belong to them, and deliver our lives from death" (Joshua 2:8-13).

First, we see Rahab's confidence and conviction in the fact of the Lord's power. Somehow, she knew what had occurred at the Red Sea and afterwards and that it was the product of the sovereign power of Israel's God. It was not merely the product of Israel's genius or some quirk of nature that parted the Red Sea. This reminds us how our lives should not only be different, but there should also be that in our lives which points to God as the reason our lives are different through the things we do and say – like going to church, our concern for people and their needs, and our specific testimony giving a reason for the hope that is within us (1 Peter 3:15-16). Second, we see Rahab's confidence and conviction in Israel's God as the One and only true God who rules Heaven and the affairs of men on earth. Her statement in verse 11, "… for the Lord your God, He is God in Heaven above and on earth beneath," is more than a statement that Israel's God was a god. The idea is that He and He alone is the true God and that He is involved with the affairs of the earth and man. This reminds us of God's involvement in our lives. He is the sovereign God who holds all things together by the word of His power, who is at work in our lives. Do we live in the light of this? Third, we see Rahab's confidence and conviction of coming judgment on her people and her desire to be delivered through aligning herself with the God of Israel (1 Peter 3:13). Note the "Now therefore …" This indicates that this request was the product of her knowledge, conviction, and faith concerning the Lord. Fourth, we see in verses

12-13 that she was not only concerned about herself. Her concern included her family or household. This is God's number one plan for evangelism, our network of family, friends, co-workers. How concerned and involved are we in our network - praying for salvation, reaching out to know and love them, and in eventually sharing the love of Christ. The inhabitants of the land were terror stricken. Three times in this chapter, the word "melted" is used to describe the emotional condition or the morale of the people (9, 11, and 24). Mentally and emotionally, they were a defeated people. God had already given the people of Jericho into their hands. This had been the case for how long? Since they had heard about the events of the Red Sea (2:9-11). The question is, did Israel know it? With the exception of Moses, Joshua, and Caleb, the people of Israel refused to believe the promise of God, instead they allowed the negative report of the ten spies to melt their hearts because they were looking at the problems rather than at their God. Note the irony here: the inhabitants were looking at Israel's God and were shaking in their sandals. The Israelites, who had seen the mighty works of God over and over again, were looking at their problems rather than God and were terrorized into unbelief.

When they returned from spying out the land, at the end of forty days, they proceeded to come to Moses and Aaron and to all the congregation of the sons of Israel in the wilderness of Paran, at Kadesh; and they brought back word to them and to all the congregation and showed them the fruit of the land. Thus, they told him, and said,

> "We went in to the land where you sent us; and it certainly does flow with milk and honey, and this is its fruit. Nevertheless, the people who live in the land are strong, and the cities are fortified and very large; and moreover, we saw the descendants of Anak there. Amalek is living in the land of the Negev and the Hittites and the Jebusites and the Amorites are living in the hill country, and the Canaanites are living by the sea and by the side of the Jordan" (Numbers 13:25-29).
> Yet you were not willing to go up, but rebelled against the command of the Lord your God; and you grumbled in your tents and said, 'Because the Lord hates us, He has brought us out of the land of Egypt to deliver us into the hand of the Amorites to destroy us. Where can we go up? Our brethren have made our hearts melt, saying, "The people are bigger and taller than we; the cities are large and fortified to heaven. And besides, we saw the sons of the Anakim there".

Then I said to you, 'Do not be shocked, nor fear them. The Lord your God who goes before you will Himself fight on your behalf, just as He did for you in Egypt before your eyes, and in the wilderness where you saw how the Lord your God carried you, just as a man carries his son, in all the way which you have walked, until you came to this place'. But for all this, you did not trust the Lord your God,...(Deuteronomy 1:26-32)".

Regardless, whether it is the bite of a mosquito or the charge of a lion, we must learn to keep our eyes on the Lord and off the problem (Hebrews 12:1-2). So, the men said to her, "Our life for yours if you do not tell this business of ours; and it shall come about when the Lord gives us the land that we will deal kindly and faithfully with you" (Joshua 2:14). Keeping quiet about their presence and refusing to inform on them would be an evidence of her faith in the Lord and good will to the people of God (Matthew 25:24).

"Then she let them down by a rope through the window, for her house was on the city wall, so that she was living on the wall. And she said to them, "Go to the hill country, lest the pursuers happen upon you, and hide yourselves there for three days, until the pursuers return. Then afterward you may go on your way. And the men said to her, we shall be free from this oath to you which you have made us swear, unless, when we come into the land, you tie this cord of scarlet thread in the window through which you let us down, and gather to yourself into the house your father and your mother and your brothers and all your father's household. And it shall come about that anyone who goes out of the doors of your house into the street, his blood shall be on his own head, and we shall be free; but anyone who is with you in the house, his blood shall be on our head, if a hand is laid on him. But if you tell this business of ours, then we shall be free from the oath which you have made us swear. And she said, "According to your words, so be it". So she sent them away, and they departed; and she tied the scarlet cord in the window" (Joshua 2:15:20).

Just before the spies left, they confirmed their agreement with Rahab: First, her house must be identified by a scarlet cord hung from the window. Second, she and her family were to remain in the house during the attack on the city. Third, the spies reassured her that they would be free of their oath guaranteeing her protection if Rahab exposed their mission.

This story was much like the deliverance experienced in the last plague God brought on Pharaoh and on Egypt when He killed the firstborn in every household, but He spared the Israelites because of the blood of the Passover lamb which had been sprinkled on the two doorposts and the lintel of their houses. Though it has not been identified as such, it seems the scarlet

225

thread was a picture of Christ. In the days of Noah, there was safety and refuge for those who entered into the door of the ark. In Egypt there was safety and refuge for those who were gathered behind the doors that were sprinkled with the blood of the Passover lamb. For you and me, there is safety and refuge from eternal judgment—but only if we enter the right door: Jesus Christ alone. As He said in John10:9, "I am the door; if anyone enters through Me, he shall be saved".

George Whitefield, the eloquent preacher of the Great Awakening in North America (1738-40), once spoke on the text, "The Door Was Shut." There were two arrogant and disrespectful young men in the congregation, and one was overheard to say to the other in mocking tones, "What if the door is shut? Another will open." Later in the sermon, the evangelist said, "It is possible that there may be someone here who is careless and self-satisfied, and says, 'What does it matter if the door is shut? Another will open!'" The two young men looked at each other in alarm! "Yes, another door will open," Whitefield concluded. "It will be the door to the bottomless pit—the door to Hell". And they

departed and came to the hill country and remained there

for three days until the pursuers returned. Now the

pursuers had sought them all along the road but had not

found them. Then the two men returned and came down

from the hill country and crossed over and came to

Joshua the son of Nun, and they related to him all that

had happened to them. And they said to Joshua, "Surely

the Lord has given all the land into our hands, and all the

inhabitants of the land, moreover, have melted away

before us." Joshua and the men of Israel saw the words

and actions of Rahab as a clear evidence of the

sovereign providence and blessing of the Lord. Note their

confidence, "Surely, the Lord has given all the land into

our hands, ..." There are some obvious lessons from this

passage:

> (1) This demonstrates God's concern and
> work to deliver one person or one family
> who will trust Him (2 Peter 3:9). It reminds
> us God knows the hearts of men and will
> lead us to them if we are only available. It
> also teaches us that the work of God must
> take place at both ends.

(2) It demonstrates God's protection and provision of His servants to enable them to carry out their calling and purpose regardless of the circumstances. The only thing that can hinder us in doing the will of God and fulfilling our calling is our own unbelief.

(3) It demonstrates how our faith should lead to action and ministry to and for others. Rahab reached out to both the spies and to her household (John 1:35-51; 4:28-29, 39).

(4) It demonstrates how God's mercy and grace overcomes His wrath through the cross. Rahab was an Amoritess and according to the Law of Moses there was to be no pity or covenant with any inhabitants—only judgment (Deuteronomy 7:2). Through her genuine faith, she became an exception.

(5) Rahab forms a type and a pledge of God's purpose to save the Gentiles who, though without hope in the world (Ephesians 2:12), could to come to God and be a partaker with Israel through faith in Christ.

(6) Rahab provides a lesson by noting the contrast with Israel as well as the other inhabitants of Jericho. It becomes a warning against the hardening of the heart in those who see and hear but fail to respond by faith. Just hearing is not enough (bible.org).

Therefore, let us fear lest, while a promise remains of entering His rest, any one of you should seem to have come short of it. For indeed we have had Good News

228

preached to us, just as they also; but the word they heard did not profit them, because it was not united by faith in those who heard (Hebrews 4:1-2)."I know that the Lord has given you the land, and that the terror of you has fallen on us, and that all the inhabitants of the land have melted away before you. "For we have heard how the Lord dried up the water of the Red Sea before you when you came out of Egypt, and what you did to the two kings of the Amorites who were beyond the Jordan, to Sihon and Og, whom you utterly destroyed. And when we heard it, our hearts melted and no courage remained in any man any longer because of you; for the Lord your God, He is God in Heaven above and on earth beneath" (Joshua 2:9-11).

> "Therefore, just as the Holy Spirit says, Today when you hear His voice, harden not your hearts as when they provoked Me, as in the day of trial in the wilderness, where your fathers tried Me by testing Me, and saw My works for forty years. Therefore I was angry with this generation, and said, They always go astray in their heart; And they did not know My ways; as I swore in My wrath, 'They shall not enter My rest" (Hebrews 3:7-11).

In a context where the apostle Paul has been discussing his ministry as an ambassador of Christ (2 Corinthians 4:1-5:20), he declares "for we walk by faith, not by sight." To walk by faith is to walk in a spirit of prayerful dependence on the Lord and His guidance. So, James encourages us, "If anyone of you lacks wisdom, let him ask of God" (James 1:5). We are always to seek God's wisdom because we need His omniscient and sovereign guidance no matter what the issue is that faces us. Later, in his epistle, James will warn against the sin of presuming on the Lord or against pursuing our own dreams and objectives apart from seeking God's leading and will (James 4:13-17). Jeremiah declared, "I know, O Lord, that a man's way is not in himself, nor is it in man who walks to direct his steps" (Jeremiah 10:23). Man does not have the wisdom or ability, nor often the will to direct his way for "There is a way which seems right to a man, but its end is the way of death" (Proverbs 14:12). Our need is to always commit our way, our objectives, our pursuits, and our responsibilities to the Lord for not only His will and wisdom, but for His enablement

(Proverbs 16:1-4, 9). The danger is that we will presume on God's grace and strike out in our own wisdom without really seeking and searching His heart and blessing while ever realizing our total inadequacy and need of His Grace.

The danger of presumption and walking by sight is amplified a hundred-fold when we consider the fact we are in an age old conflict with supernatural forces that are extremely cunning and many times more powerful than are we. We see the material world, we see flesh and blood, and we can see the physical evidence and think, "I can handle it ... it's not that difficult." We must be ever wary because often we are not just dealing with just flesh and blood. Rather, we are dealing with an insidious enemy who uses people to promote his schemes. When we consider our weakness and Satan's power, cunning, deception, and methods of operations, we must certainly listen to Paul's admonition in Ephesians 6:10-18:

> "Finally, be strengthened in the Lord
> and in the strength of his power. Clothe
> yourselves with the full armor of God so
> that you may be able to stand against the
> schemes of the devil. For our struggle is not

against flesh and blood, but against the rulers, against the powers, against the world-rulers of this darkness, against the spiritual forces of evil in the heavens. For this reason, take up the full armor of God so that you may be able to stand your ground on the evil day, and having done everything, to stand. Stand firm, therefore, by fastening the belt of truth around your waist, by putting on the breastplate of righteousness, by fitting your feet with the preparation that comes from the good news of peace, and in all of this, by taking up the shield of faith with which you can extinguish all the flaming arrows of the evil one. And take the helmet of salvation and the sword of the Spirit, which is the word of God. With every prayer and petition, pray at all times in the Spirit, and to this end being alert, with all perseverance and requests for all the saints. Pray for me, that I may be given the message when I begin to speak - that I may confidently make known the mystery of the gospel, for which I am an ambassador in chains. Pray that I may be able to speak boldly as I ought to speak" (Ephesians 6:10-20).

In chapter nine, though somewhat cautious, Joshua nevertheless failed to inquire of the Lord through prayer. Looking at the evidence, he supposed he could wisely discern what they were facing. He was wrong and ultimately; he was guilty of presuming on the Lord.

In this passage of scripture, we see the danger of failing to commit our way to the Lord (Proverbs 3:5-

7; Psalms 37:4-6), the peril of prayerlessness and the peril of walking by sight - making decision on the basis of how things appear. As we have seen, Israel's failure at Ai was to a large degree the result of failing to consult the Lord. Now again the failure of the leaders to commit their way to the Lord was about to produce another crisis. It reminds us again how susceptible we are to acting before praying. There is another related problem here. The problem of trusting in our victories and our religious experiences. The context here is most significant. The people had just returned from a mountain-top kind of spiritual experience after hearing the Word of God read to them from Mt. Ebal and Mt. Gerizim. They had heard God's promises of blessings and had affirmed their commitment to follow the Lord (Deuteronomy 27:11-28:14). It had been a time of spiritual victory, a spiritual high, but this is an important time for walking circumspectly knowing that such is also a time when often Satan attacks because he knows we are apt to trust in our experiences rather than in the Lord (1 Corinthians 10:12). The moment we let down our guard and think we have it made because of our spiritual experiences; we are most vulnerable to the devil's attacks. The judgment of God's word here is that they "... did not ask for counsel of the Lord" (9:14). As we study this passage we should be reminded of four passages of Scripture 1 Samuel 12:23; Proverbs 3:5-6; 1 Corinthians 10:12; Ephesians 6:10-18. These verses along with this passage in Joshua remind us of four things:

> (1) "As Christians, we are involved in deadly spiritual warfare with a power far superior to our own strength.
>
> (2) To be delivered from our opponent and his nefarious schemes, we must cloth ourselves with our spiritual armor as given us in Christ.
>
> (3) The offensive weapons given to us by the Lord are the Word of God and prayer. Without the Word and prayer, we are sitting ducks.
>
> (4) When God's people are victorious or are prospered, it seems Satan doubles his efforts in attacks against them. Now when all the kings west of the Jordan heard about these things—those in the hill country, in the western foothills, and along the entire coast of the Great Sea as far as Lebanon (the kings of the Hittites, Amorites, Canaanites, Perizzites, Hivites and Jebusites) they came together to make war against Joshua and Israel" (bible.org).

The record given here is typical of Satan's strategies. Powerful alliances began immediately to form in both the north and the south of Canaan. Where tribal warfare had gone on for years, suddenly deadly enemies were brought together in alliances as they united against the invasion of God's people into the land. When righteousness becomes aggressive and bent on an objective, it has a way of uniting the forces of righteousness and the enemies of righteousness. It happened this way when Jesus Christ launched his earthly ministry. His aggressive ministry of healing, preaching, and the confrontation of sin galvanized his own followers—but it also welded together three groups which had formerly been enemies, the Pharisees, the Sadducees, and the Herodians. Scripture predicts that His future return will have a similar effect (Psalm 2:2; Revelation19:19.)

The more boldly the Christian faith advances, the more vocal and violent the opposition will become. It appears that all the city-states in mountainous regions joined forces against Israel as a means of keeping Joshua and his army from attacking one city at a time as had been done with Jericho and Ai. Perhaps these kings were encouraged by the initial defeat of Israel at Ai. No longer would the reports of earlier victories lead them to suppose that Israel was invincible. In resisting Israel, however, they were resisting God. Their stubborn rebellion against God was eloquent testimony that the sin of the Amorites had reached its full measure (Genesis 15:16).

"When the residents of Gibeon heard what Joshua did to Jericho and Ai, they did something clever. They collected some provisions and put worn out sacks on their donkeys, along with worn out wineskins that were ripped and patched. They had worn out, patched sandals on their feet and dressed in worn out clothes. All their bread was dry and hard. They came to Joshua at the camp in Gilgal and said to him and the men of Israel, we have come from a distant land. Make a treaty with us. The men of Israel said to the Hivites, Perhaps you live near us. So how can we make a treaty with you? But they said to Joshua, we are willing to be your subjects. So Joshua said to them, who are you and where do you come from? They told him, your subjects have come from a very distant land because of the reputation of the Lord your God, for we have heard the news about all he did in

236

Egypt and all he did to the two Amorite kings on the other side of the Jordan - Sihon king of Heshbon and Og king of Bashan in Ashtaroth. Our leaders and all who live in our land told us, take provisions for your journey and go meet them. Tell them, we are willing to be your subjects. Make a treaty with us. This bread of ours was warm when we packed it in our homes the day we started out to meet you, but now it is dry and hard. These wineskins we filled were brand new, but look how they have ripped. Our clothes and sandals have worn out because it has been a very long journey. The men examined some of their provisions, but they failed to ask the Lord's advice. Joshua made a peace treaty with them and agreed to let them live. The leaders of the community sealed it with an oath. Not all were willing to openly go against Israel in view of Israel's victories" (bible.org).

The Gibeonites, which included a league of cities, concocted a clever ruse designed to deceive the Israelites and hide their true identity – a typical strategy of Satan, the deceiver. Their goal, which was successful, was to convince the Israelites they were from a country outside the land. They evidently somehow knew that God had commanded the Israelites to totally destroy all the inhabitants of the land. Their claim was that they were impressed with the great things Joshua had done and so they wanted a treaty allowing them to live because they

were not of the land of Canaan. It is hard not to admire

the Gibeonites for their scheme. In view of verse 9, it

appears they really did believe in the power of the God of

Israel much like Rahab. The Gibeonites were not

cowards (10:2). They knew they could not withstand the

power of God and did the next best thing in their thinking;

they turned to deception through disguise. This resulted

in major approaches:

> (1) "They played on their sympathies by
> appearing as weary travelers who had been
> on a long journey. Their garments were
> dirty and worn, their food was dry and
> moldy (or hard, crumbly), their wineskins
> old and patched, and their sandals worn
> and thin.
> (2) They played on their egos and their
> sense of pride. They insisted they came
> from a great distance to show their respect
> for the power of the God of the Israelites
> and wanted to be allowed to live as the
> servants of Israel. Caught off guard, Joshua
> and the leaders of Israel listened to the ruse
> of the Gibeonites and they made two
> mistakes:
>
> (3) They made the mistake of allowing the
> Gibeonites to play on their emotions. They
> accepted the evidence, though
> questionable, without further and more
> reliable evidence. Here we see the peril of
> sight versus faith and fact.

(4) The primary mistake, however, is not seeking counsel from the Lord. They should have sought direction from the Lord through the Urim and Thummim. Here we see the peril of presumption through prayerlessness. It is always a mistake for us to lean on our own wisdom or judgment and make our own plans apart from God's direction. It was a mistake then ... and it still is. The exhortation of God's Word is: Trust in the Lord with all your heart, And do not lean on your own understanding. In all your ways acknowledge Him, And He will make your paths straight. Do not be wise in your own eyes; Fear the Lord and turn away from evil (Proverbs 3:5-7). Before entering into any alliance—taking a partner in life, going into business with another, yielding assent to any proposition which involves confederation with others—be sure to ask counsel at the mouth of the Lord. He will assuredly answer by an irresistible impulse—by the voice of a friend; by a circumstance strange and unexpected; by a passage of Scripture. He will choose His own messenger; but He will send a message" (bible.org).

Though Satan surely knows he can never really defeat the Lord and that he is a defeated foe, he nevertheless turns to his many tricks and deceptive devices to defeat God's purposes for and with His people (Ephesians 4:14; 2 Timothy 2:25). Three days after they made the treaty with them, the Israelites found out they were from the local area and lived nearby. And they set out and on the third day arrived at their cities - Gibeon, Kephirah, Beeroth, and Kiriath Jearim. Within only three days the deception was discovered, but as is often the case with the consequences of sin, they would live with their decision for the rest of their lives. Proverbs 12:19 is pertinent here which says, "Truthful lips will be established forever, But a lying tongue is only for a moment". Words of truth are consistent, and stand all tests, while lies are soon discovered and exposed. The Israelites did not attack them because the leaders of the community had sworn an oath to them in the name of the Lord God of Israel. The whole community criticized the leaders, but all the leaders told the whole community: "We swore an oath to them in the name of the Lord God of Israel. So now we can't hurt them. We must let them live so we can escape the curse attached to the oath we swore to them". The leaders then added, "Let them live". So they became woodcutters and water carriers for the whole community, as the leaders had decided. Joshua summoned the Gibeonites and said to them, "Why did you trick us by saying, 'We live far away from you,' when you really live nearby"? Now you are condemned to perpetual servitude as woodcutters and water carriers for the house of my God". They said to Joshua, "It was carefully reported to your subjects how the Lord your God commanded Moses his servant to assign you the whole land and to destroy all who live in the land from before you. Because of you we were terrified we would lose our lives, so we did this thing. So now we are in your power. Do to us what you think is good and appropriate". Joshua did as they said, he kept the Israelites from killing them and that day made them woodcutters and water carriers for the community and for the altar of the Lord at the divinely chosen site. (They continue in this capacity to this very day.)

The text tells us that once the ruse was discovered, the people grumbled against their leaders because they judged them to be responsible. However, though they erred by leaning on their own understanding rather than consulting the Lord, they honored their agreement with the Gibeonites. Had they not been men of honor and integrity, they might easily have sought to cover their tracks by destroying the Gibeonites, but they honored their pledge because it had been ratified in the name of Yahweh, the God of Israel. To break the covenant would dishonor God's name and bring down His wrath. "In fact, such a judgment from God would later come to pass during David's reign because Saul disregarded this agreement". (2 Samuel 21:1-6) While they could not go back on their pledge, the Gibeonites had deceived them, so a punishment fitting their sin had to be prescribed. First, Joshua rebuked them for their dishonesty and then sentenced them to perpetual slavery. In the ruse of the Gibeonites, they had offered to be the subjects of the Israelites (2 Samuel 21:8,11). By this they were merely offering to become Israel's vassals. In return they expected Israel, the stronger of the two, to protect them from their enemies (2 Samuel10:6). This backfires on them and they had to become Israel's slaves. They would become woodcutters and water-bearers for the Israelites, especially in relation to the tabernacle service. In God's grace, this turned out to be a great blessing....to keep the Gibeonites' idolatry from defiling the true faith of Israel, their work would be carried out in the tabernacle, where they would be exposed to the worship of the one true God. As a result, the very thing the Gibeonites hoped to retain—their freedom—was lost. But the curse eventually became a blessing. It was on behalf of the Gibeonites that God later worked a great miracle (Joshua 10:10-14). Later, the tabernacle of the Lord would be pitched at Gibeon (2 Chronicles 1:30, and the Gibeonites (later known as Nethinims) would replace the Levites in temple service (Ezra 2:43 and 8:20). That is the amazing way the grace of God works. He is still able to turn a curse into a blessing. While it is true that the natural consequences of our sin generally have to run their course, God in His grace not only forgives but in many cases, He actually overrules our mistakes and brings blessing out of sin. In Joshua 9:27 we read, "... and that day made them woodcutters and water carriers for the community and for the altar of the Lord at the divinely chosen site". (They continue in this capacity to this very day). How tremendous and gracious of God. They had the privilege of being brought close to the Lord and spiritual things on a regular basis. It is interesting that in later years, when the Israelites would go into idolatry, the Gibeonites would still be standing at the altar where the true God ordained those sacrifices should be made for sins. As a result of what they had seen God do for Israel, they became convinced, like Rahab, that Israel's God was the true God. Like Rahab, they evidently became loyal Believers. For many years after this incident, there was war between the citizens of the land and the invading Israelites. Yet never once in the record of that long conquest do we hear of any Gibeonite defecting to his original side.

CHAPTER 10

THE TIME IS NOW TO SEE YOUR TODAY IN YOUR TOMORROW

Sometimes in life, trials and tribulations can make us so weak that we become unconcerned with the greatness that God has promised that He have in store for us. We give up the fight and we lay down and die, and the enemy rejoices because he believes that we are out for the count. But I declare today that the feeling of defeat will no long reside in me or you. We must continue to fight, we must continue to fast and pray, and we can watch God manifest victory in our lives. What I go through today will not dictate my tomorrow. One of my favorite scripture's states, "Weeping may endure for a night, but joy cometh in the morning", (Psalm 30:5). I believe the main thing that keeps us from seeing all that God has in store for us is our blurred vision. I know many people can argue that they have 20/20, but how is your spiritual vision. One of my favorite stories in the Bible is when Elisha and his servant were being surrounded by the Syrians. When the servant saw the enemy, he saw defeat.

> The Bible states in 2 Kings 6:15:" And when the servant of the man of God was risen early, and gone forth behold, an host compassed the city both with horses and chariots. And his servant said unto him, Alas, my master! How shall we do!"

The servant's reaction was indication to me that it was not visible to him that the Lord was on their side, the only thing that he could see was the mass of people coming for them. That is how we can get so often in life, we don't see God's hand, but we see all the bad things that come at us. Our mind does not go back to how God delivered us out of so many other snares, we just always focus on the snare before us. Our vision is so blurred. When Elisha heard his servant utter those words, He immediately gave him a glimpse of what he saw through his spiritual eyes by saying, "And he answered, Fear not; for they that be with us are more than they that be with them" (2 Kings 6:16). That's how we should look are our obstacles, He who is with me is bigger than any attack that can come against me. And Elisha, who was not a selfish leader, didn't want to be the only one on his team to see God's awesome power, he wanted his servant to be able to see it too. So, what does the man of God do? He begins to pray. 2 Kings 2:17:

> "And Elisha prayed, and said, Lord, I pray thee, open his eyes, that he may see. And the Lord opened the eyes of the young man; and he saw; and behold, the mountain was full of horses and chariots of fire round about Elisha". Then and only then was the servant able to see.

In ministry, God has shown be some amazing things and to be quite honest, some of the things that God revealed to me scared even me. And I get before the church and I declare everything that God has shown me, and I can see pass the congregation shouting "Amen" and "I see that Pastor", to know that a lot of things that God give me they really do not see. I have to get in a place of prayer and ask God to open their eyes. Even if God may use me to prophesy that God is getting ready to bless them with a house, or a car, or even a better mind, many will let their current circumstance hinder them from seeing and receiving the prophetic word that God used me to release. In return I have to pray, God open their eyes so that they can see their today in their tomorrow. If people can tap into that simple act, I believe their love for God would be different, and I also believe their actions toward God would be so different. I have a young man in the ministry. When I first started dealing with him, he was in jail with long hair and gold teeth. Every time he saw me, I continued to preach sound doctrine because I knew if he could ever see past his circumstance God had so much better for him. One day after jail ministry he walked up to me and told me that as soon as he was released from jail, he was going to find me and attend the church I Pastor. I had heard that promise so many times, but there was something so different about him. He was eventually released from jail, and he made good on his word, he came and joined the church. As part of his release, he had to be placed on house arrest as well as probation. Sometimes we would have a church service at another location and because he was on house arrest he would have to go before his probation officer to request to go to church with us.

Sometimes they allowed him to go and, sometimes they denied him. Often times I would be preaching, and I would see the probation officer sitting in the back of the church watching this young man, and I could see the discouragement written all over his face. Even with all of that against him, he remained faithful, he did not do everything right all the time, but he had an earnest strive. One day while he was cleaning the church with my wife, he made mention that he was ready to get married and have a family. As a result of him continuing to stay faithful to God even when all odds were against him, God sent him a wife. A young lady from another church came one day just to visit, and they began to talk. Six months later they were married. During their courtship, we told them, not to kiss, or even be alone with each other. We would drive him in one car, and she would be in another. But I watched God manifest himself in that young man's life. Now he is preaching the gospel, he is a business owner, and he and his wife are raising their beautiful children. In everything that he went through, he chose to see his today in his tomorrow. He used every hindrance as a stepping stone, and if you look at him now, he doesn't even look close to what he has been through. I have another man of God that was on crack cocaine for thirty years, and now he is completely drug free preaching the gospel. Then there was another that had all types of gun charges and was on probation, I went to court with him, spoke on his behalf and now he is serving faithfully in the ministry. Those men of God saw their today in their tomorrow, and they made it!

I was studying one day and came across a particular scripture in the book of Joshua (which prompt me to use this particular title for this chapter) and it wasn't a long scripture, but it was indeed a powerful scripture. Joshua 3:5 reads: "And Joshua said unto the people, Sanctify yourselves: for to morrow the Lord will do wonders among you." I looked at that scripture over and over and over again. I began to say, it's so powerful that how I choose to act today can dictate what I receive tomorrow. Wow! If I am willing to obey God's word today, makes me eligible for a blessing on tomorrow. Now that alone causes for a praise break. Many people only live for today as if there is no tomorrow, but now is the time for me to see my today in my tomorrow. By the people of God choosing to sanctify (giving themselves a thorough cleaning) themselves, they opened themselves up to receive wonders. I am often in the midst of many congregations, and I hear a preacher bellow out, "When praises go up, blessing come down", and it seems so crazy. After that word is released, I see some that grasp that concept while others just sit with their hands folded waiting on the next order of program. But that saying is so true, what you do today can be beneficial for you tomorrow if and only if you are willing to do something.

In my summary, I am reminded of John 3:16: "For God so loved the world, that he gave His only begotten Son, that whosoever believeth on Him should not perish, but have everlasting life". As I stated earlier, my life did not truly begin, until I humbly submitted to the will of God. Through the preaching of the gospel, and by calling on the name of Jesus; my life has been transformed. I am a living example of how God can bring you up from the 'least to the greatest'. So, hold on, don't quit, because the best is still yet to come.

BIBLIOGRAPHY

Dictionary of the Old Testament: The Pentateuch: Downers Grove, Ill: InterVarsity, 2003.

http://biblehub.com/sermons/auth/rowlands/the_biography_of_enoch.htm (the life of Enoch

https://bible.org/seriespage/2-preparing-enter-land-joshua-21-24

http://biblescripture.net/KJV and NIV

http://flowerheaven.wordpress.com/2011/02/12/king-david-a-man-after-gods-own-heart/

https://landerroark.wordpress.com/2015/04/20/we-must-believe/

http://overviewbible.com/hebrews/

http://thelife.com/challenges/practicing-patience-when-god-has-you-waiting

http://www.gotquestions.org/life-David.html

http://www.gotquestions.org/thelifeof-Joseph.html

http://www.lifeissues.net/writers/gro/gro_110painofrejection.html

http://www.oneplace.com/howtopraiseyourwaytovictory.html

Lindsay, Gordon, <u>The Life and Teachings of Christ</u>.
Christ for the Nations, Inc. 16th Printing, 2009, page 44.

Lucado, Max, <u>Traveling Light: Releasing the Burdens you Were Never Intended to Bear</u>. Waterville, ME: Walker, 2003, page 14.

MacArthur, John, <u>Twelve Ordinary Men</u>. Nashville, Tennessee: Thomas Nelson, 2005, page 32 and 75.

Maxwell, John C.,<u>Running with the Giants. What Old Testament Heroes Want You to Know About Life and Leadership</u>. First Hachette Book Group Edition: September, 2002, pages 29 and 30.

<u>NLT Study Bible The Truth Made Clear</u>. Tyndale House Publishers, Inc. 2007.